Beyond Banksters
Resisting the New Feudalism

by Joyce Nelson

Design by Ester Strijbos
Cover photograph by Adrian Berg

Printed and bound in Victoria, British Columbia, Canada.

Watershed Sentinel Books
Box 1270,
Comox, B.C. Canada
V9M 7Z8

www.watershedsentinel.ca

To order: *www.watershedsentinel.ca/banksters*

Library and Archives Canada Cataloguing in Publication

Nelson, Joyce, 1945-, author
Beyond Banksters : Resisting the New Feudalism/Joyce Nelson

Includes bibliographical references and index.
ISBN 978-0-9953286-0-0 (paperback)

1. Bank of Canada. 2. Banks and banking—Corrupt practices—Canada.
3. Debts, Public—Canada. 4. Privatization. 5. International trade. 6. Bankruptcy.
I. Title.

HG1573.N44 2016
332.1   C2016-906428-X

Beyond Banksters explores how the powers of the Bank of Canada were appropriated in the 1970s, resulting in billions of dollars in public debt. It explores how the BOC lawsuit is now being undermined by Justin Trudeau's Liberal government. That government is planning to greatly increase Canada's sovereign debt through $120 billion in infrastructure spending, with the money borrowed from investors by a new Canada Infrastructure Bank.

In telling that factual story, this book also lifts the curtain on little-known aspects of recent history, including the financial industry's involvement in the brutal crackdown on Occupy Wall Street; the PR campaign to "save capitalism" since 2011; the banks profiting from the sell-off of Ontario's Hydro One; the bankrupting of Iceland and its fight back; Bilderberg and the targeting of Denmark for electricity privatization; and the ruinous pending trade deals that threaten any attempts to regulate the banks. As the reader will see, all of these aspects are directly connected to major financial players – like the Bank for International Settlements, McKinsey & Company, BlackRock, and Bilderberg – who are orchestrating our future.

Beyond Banksters also explores postal banking, public banking, and various ways in which people are resisting the postmodern serfdom being imposed on societies everywhere. From Milton Friedman to Trudeau's Canada Infrastructure Bank, from BlackRock to crappy trade deals to Bilderberg, *Beyond Banksters* exposes the major players privatizing the world and creating a new state of feudalism. Iceland resisted and so can we.

Reviews for *Beyond Banksters: Resisting The New Feudalism*

"Always cutting edge, writer Joyce Nelson has penned a chilling dissection of the hidden-in-plain-view takeover of Canada by a global economic elite and their Banksters. The tightening noose of foreign economic domination that serves the billionaire class is choking off Canada's very sovereignty. Ms. Nelson brilliantly exposes this crisis in a wakeup call that reads like a spy thriller. Unfortunately, this is not fiction but reality, the sober, blunt truth that politicians and the mainstream media spin and hide. If you care about your economic future, read this book and act."

— John Stauber, author of *Toxic Sludge Is Good For You* and *Weapons of Mass Deception*

"A powerful and chilling investigation into an emerging global oligarchy of banks and corporations. Acutely insightful, Beyond Banksters digs deep into the nature of this new order and its repressive and impoverishing effects, while also revealing possibilities for resistance and change. Written with wit and clarity, Beyond Banksters is not only informative but a pleasure to read."

— Joel Bakan, Professor of Law, University of British Columbia, and author of *The Corporation: The Pathological Pursuit of Profit and Power* and *Childhood Under Siege: How Big Business Targets Your Children*

In the political confusion, "What's needed is a focal point – a sort of history and playbook combination, a reference point – and Beyond Banksters has provided this brilliantly. With eminently readable, short chapters, free of jargon, this very fine book by prominent Canadian author Joyce Nelson is a must for anyone who wants to understand what's happening."

— Rafe Mair, Broadcaster, co-founder of The Common Sense Canadian, *www.commonsensecanadian.ca*

"Read this book, and then help put a stop to the on-going rip-off. Your children and grandchildren will thank you."

— Anne Cameron, author of *Dreamspeaker*

"This well researched book sheds new light on what is really going on in the financial world, and anyone who cares about Canada would be well advised to read it."

— Hon. Paul Hellyer, former Minister of National Defence

"Hard hitting, well researched, succinct, fast paced, Beyond Banksters lays bare the usually hidden world of Canadian and international bankers. Want to know how to disentangle the web of banks buying up and privatizing Canada's public assets? Read Beyond Banksters and learn about the central players and their cozy relations with governments and international fraudsters. Written by one of Canada's best freelance investigative writers, this is a hopeful book, offering attractive alternatives to rule by banksters."

— Gordon Laxer, author of *After the Sands: Energy and Ecological Security for Canadians*

"Provocative, profound, challenging and suffused with perceptive clarity, Beyond Banksters: Resisting the New Feudalism will doubtless elicit joy from those who agree and rage from those who don't – precisely what we expect from this gadfly extraordinaire."

— Stephen Hume, author, Vancouver Sun columnist

"Read it and then get your Member of Parliament to read it."

— Duncan Cameron, Centre for Global Political Economy, Simon Fraser University

Table of Contents:

Introduction

I didn't have an extra $1,500 lying around at the time, so in late July 2014 when I saw ads for the big "Canada Summit" scheduled for December 3, 2014 in Toronto, I didn't order a ticket. Had I known that less than two years later I'd be writing this book, I would have scrounged up the money. Many bigwigs were scheduled to speak: Frank McKenna, Deputy Chair of TD Bank and Chair of Brookfield Asset Management; Ron Mock, CEO of Ontario Teachers' Pension Plan; Ed Clark, CEO of TD Bank; David Miller, CEO and President of WWF Canada; Diane Francis, author of *Merger of the Century: Why Canada and America Should Become One Country*; and many more.

The "Canada Summit 2014: Confronting the Big Questions" had been organized by *The Economist* to bring together business executives and government leaders to "discuss Canada's economic future and identify new areas of opportunity."

The panel that really caught my eye was one called "The Global Banking Picture," because it was addressing questions like this: "What should be the role of the Bank of Canada going forward in the post-Mark Carney era?" I knew that the Bank of Canada is our central bank and it is publicly owned, so it struck me as odd that the four panelists scheduled to discuss this question were from the Desjardins Group, the International Monetary Fund (IMF), the Bank of Tokyo Canada, and JP Morgan Chase Canada.

The simple questions that crossed my mind at the time were: Why are private investment bankers and the IMF discussing the future of the Bank of Canada? Isn't that something that should be addressed by Members of Parliament and all Canadians, rather than the banksters?

I also noticed that the promotional material for the 2014 Summit was telling people that "Canada's stable macroeconomic environment and sound monetary policy allowed it to emerge from the global financial crisis barely scathed." But economist David Macdonald had revealed in 2012 that there had been "secret bank bailouts" of Canada's top six banks amounting to at least $108 billion and likely as much as $114 billion between September 2008 and July 2010.

Macdonald's report, published by the Canadian Centre for Policy Alternatives, disproved "the repeated claims that Canadian banks did not receive massive government support during the recent financial meltdown. Nothing could be further from the truth," he wrote.[1]

Macdonald delivered some shocking figures: for example, while TD Bank was receiving $26 billion dollars in taxpayer bailout money, "Ed Clark of TD had his overall compensation raised from $11.1 million to $15.2 million" per year. Other banks that received "extraordinary support" included Royal Bank of Canada ($23 billion), Scotiabank ($23 billion), CIBC ($21 billion), BMO ($17 billion) and National Bank ($3 billion).[2]

A spokesman for then-Finance Minister Jim Flaherty had responded to the report by saying, "Despite conspiracy theories to the contrary, there was no 'secret bailout'." But as one reporter noted at the time, "To some extent the report and the rebuttal to it are a matter of how the facts are interpreted. Where Macdonald says 'bailout,' a finance ministry official says 'liquidity support'."[3]

So when I noticed that the Canada Summit 2014 promotional materials were calling Canada "barely scathed" by the global financial crisis, it seemed as odd as having banksters and the IMF discussing the future of the Bank of Canada.

Looking back, I'd say that NOT going to that 2014 Canada Summit was the genesis for this book, because that's when I started researching to answer my own financial questions. As a writer, for the past several years I'd mainly focused on environmental issues and if you had asked me to name my favourite economist, I would have answered – George Carlin. I like people who explain things without jargon.

Subsequently, I've discovered Michael Hudson and Michel Chossudovsky, and I've become fond of financial writers like Ellen Brown, Pat Martens and Russ Martens, Matt Taibbi, Paul Hellyer, Jim Stanford, Michael Lewis and others who can cut through bafflegab terms like "liquidity support."

What some of those writers and others are now warning about is neofeudalism and the rise of an elite class of multi-millionaire financiers and billionaires.

Neofeudalism

As Chris Hedges writes, "A handful of corporate oligarchs around the world now have everything – wealth, power and privilege – while the rest of us struggle as a part of a vast underclass, increasingly impoverished and ruthlessly repressed."[4] David Rosen calls this "postmodern serfdom," imposed through income inequality and austerity measures that are incrementally (or otherwise) moving entire societies to "perpetual economic and social poverty."[5]

In her 2015 piece called "Plutocracy Awaits Us," Linda McQuaig notes that income inequality in Canada is not yet as extreme as elsewhere, but we are relentlessly moving in the same direction.[6]

In fact, a 2005 report by banking giant Citigroup had already identified Canada as a "plutonomy" – a country with "massive income and wealth inequality," where "the rich are likely to keep getting even richer."[7]

A massive part of the problem is what's called "sovereign debt," the debt that national governments owe because of their borrowing from private lenders – even though they have the power to issue the national money supply themselves. Mystified by the bank lobbyists and right-wing economists, misinformed legislators (or outright collaborators) have saddled their nations with so much needless debt that their people are enslaved by it.

As Ellen Brown explains, sovereign debt around the globe "has ballooned from \$89 trillion to \$100 trillion just since 2008. Squeezed governments have been driven to radical austerity measures, privatizing public assets, slashing public services, and downsizing work forces in a futile attempt to balance national budgets. But the debt overhang just continues to grow."[8]

Judy Kennedy has observed, "When people are held hostage financially they can be easily controlled. Public programs can be eliminated, services cut, and the economy downgraded while billions are siphoned through the banks to the 1%."[9] That kind of financial hostage-taking also induces governments to ruin the environment, sacrificing whole regions mainly to benefit the oligarchs. George Monbiot states that the many environmental crises we face "cannot be won without a wider political fight: a democratic mobilisation against plutocracy."[10]

In fact, the phrase "sovereign debt" is actually an oxymoron. As Brown puts it (in a column about Brexit), "A government oppressed by 'sovereign' debt is not really sovereign. A sovereign government has the power to issue money and need not go into debt at all. But EU member governments have lost that sovereign power. They are unable to issue their own money or borrow money issued by their own central banks."[11] Thus, EU members are forced to borrow from private investment banks and increase their ever-ballooning sovereign debt.

As a result, almost without anyone noticing, banks have become far, far more than banks. By using all that compound interest paid to them by governments, they are literally buying up everything that can return a profit. Matt Taibbi wrote in 2014, "Today banks like Morgan Stanley, JP Morgan Chase and Goldman Sachs own oil tankers, run airports and control huge quantities of coal, natural gas, heating oil, electric power and precious metals. They likewise can now be found exerting direct control over the supply of a whole galaxy of raw materials crucial to world industry and to society in general, including everything from food products to metals like zinc, copper, tin, nickel, and...aluminum."[12]

Peter Phillips and Brady Osborne recently wrote, "The transnational capitalist class is laying the foundation for the privatization of the world," gradually creating "neo-feudal societies" where "the people serve as peasants."[13]

"Break up the banks," said Bernie Sanders, and millions agreed. The need to scale back the power of the banks has become obvious.

That's where Canada is in a unique position: we still have a publicly-owned central bank, the Bank of Canada (BOC), which has the power to issue money and near-zero interest loans to our federal and provincial governments without incurring debt to private lenders. Indeed, the BOC did that successfully for 35 years, from 1938 to 1974 – within the memory of living Canadians – while transforming the country in positive ways.

The Bank of Canada Lawsuit

In part, this book is about the ongoing lawsuit launched by the Toronto-based Committee on Monetary and Economic Reform (COMER) seeking to require the BOC to return to its original mandate. COMER's

Herb Wiseman calls the BOC "part of the Civil Commons" which has been "appropriated by the financial elite" to run up huge "sovereign debt" and deficits since 1974.[14] Long-time journalist Ed Finn has called this part of "the biggest financial scam that was ever conceived."[15] Writer Murray Dobbin considers the undermining and appropriation of the Bank of Canada "far and away the biggest, most outrageous fraud ever perpetrated on the Canadian people."[16]

Beyond Banksters explores how that appropriation happened, and how the BOC lawsuit is now being undermined by Justin Trudeau's Liberal government. That government is planning to greatly increase Canada's sovereign debt through $120 billion in infrastructure spending, with the money borrowed from investors by a new Canada Infrastructure Bank.

In telling that factual story, this book also lifts the curtain on little-known aspects of recent history, including the financial industry's involvement in the brutal crackdown on Occupy Wall Street; the PR campaign to "save capitalism" since 2011; the banks profiting from the sell-off of Ontario's Hydro One; the bankrupting of Iceland and its fight back; Bilderberg and the targeting of Denmark for electricity privatization; and the ruinous pending trade deals that threaten any attempts to regulate the banks. As the reader will see, all of these aspects are directly connected to major financial players – like the Bank for International Settlements, McKinsey & Company, BlackRock, and Bilderberg – who are orchestrating our future.

Beyond Banksters also explores postal banking, public banking, and various ways in which people resist the "postmodern serfdom" being imposed on societies everywhere. COMER and its lawsuit are inspiring many around the world to take back their governments' monetary powers.

In January 2016, *Watershed Sentinel* magazine published the first entry in this book, "The Bank of Canada Lawsuit," as a feature also posted on its website. Over the past nine months (to September), that article has been read by more than 151,000 people – suggesting that there may be interest out there in learning more about these issues. I have added a few words (and footnotes) to that article, but otherwise left it intact.

I am pleased to have this book see the light of day, and to work with Delores Broten as its editor and Watershed Sentinel Books as publisher. Other acknowledgements can be found at the end of the book.

1. The Bank of Canada Lawsuit

One of the most important legal cases in Canadian history is slowly inching its way towards trial. Launched in 2011 by the Toronto-based Committee on Monetary and Economic Reform (COMER), the lawsuit would require the publicly-owned Bank of Canada to return to its pre-1974 mandate and practice of lending nearly interest-free money to federal, provincial and (potentially) municipal governments for infrastructure and healthcare spending.

Renowned constitutional lawyer Rocco Galati has taken on the case for COMER, and he considers it his most important case to date.[1]

On October 14, 2015, a Federal Court judge cleared away yet another legal roadblock thrown in the lawsuit's path. The federal government has tried to quash the case as frivolous and "hypothetical," but the courts keep allowing it to proceed. As Galati maintains, "The case is on sound legal and constitutional grounds."

When asked after the October procedural hearing why Canadians should care about the case, Galati quickly responded: "Because they're paying $30 or $40 billion a year in useless interest. Since '74, more than a trillion to fraudsters, that's why they should care." (COMER says the figures are closer to $60 billion per year, and $2 trillion since 1974.)

The Fraudsters

Created during the Great Depression, the Bank of Canada funded a wide range of public infrastructure projects from 1938 to 1974, without our governments incurring debt to private lenders. Projects like the Trans-Canada highway system, the St. Lawrence Seaway, universities, hospitals, ports and airports were all funded by interest-free loans from the Bank of Canada. In addition, universal medicare, old-age pensions, and tuition-free postsecondary education were all made possible by Bank of Canada funding.[2]

But in 1974, the Liberal government of Pierre Trudeau was quietly seduced into joining the Bank for International Settlements (BIS) – the powerful private Swiss-based bank which oversees (private) central banks across the planet. The BIS insisted on a crucial change in Canada.

According to Murray Dobbin, in 1974 the BIS's new Basel Committee – supposedly in order to establish global financial "stability" – strongly encouraged governments "to borrow from private lenders and end the practice of borrowing interest-free from their own central banks. The rationale was thin from the start. Central bank borrowing was and is no more inflationary than borrowing through the private banks. The only difference was that private banks were given the legal right to fleece Canadians."[3]

And that's exactly what "the fraudsters" did. After 1974, the Bank of Canada stopped lending to federal and provincial governments and forced them to borrow from private and foreign lenders at compound interest rates – resulting in huge deficits and debts ever since. Just paying off the accumulated compound interest – called "servicing the debt" – is a significant part of every provincial and federal budget. In Ontario, for example, debt-servicing charges amounted to some $11.4 billion for the year 2015.

What is key to the COMER lawsuit is that the Bank of Canada is still a public central bank (the only one left among G7 countries). Their lawsuit seeks to "restore the use of the Bank of Canada to its original purpose, by exercising its public statutory duty and responsibility. That purpose includes making interest-free loans to the municipal, provincial, and federal governments for 'human capital' expenditures (education, health, and other social services) and/or infrastructure expenditures."

Deliberate Obfuscation

In February 2015, Rocco Galati stated publicly: "I have a firm basis to believe that the [federal] government has requested or ordered the mainstream media not to cover this [COMER] case." Subsequently, the *Toronto Star* and the CBC both gave the lawsuit some coverage in spring 2015 and there was good coverage in alternative media in Canada. But given the importance of infrastructure spending in the federal election campaign later that year, it's amazing (and sad) that the COMER lawsuit was so ignored, even by the political parties – especially the NDP.

With the Harper government touting its ten-year $14 billion Building Canada Fund, and the Liberal Party of Justin Trudeau promising to at least double that amount of funding by running three years of deficits, the NDP led by Tom Mulcair pledged to balance the budget. The NDP could have explained and championed the COMER lawsuit and even possibly utilized it to somehow justify its balanced-budget promise – an austerity platform plank that likely cost it the election.

In August 2015, Justin Trudeau spoke vaguely about financing infrastructure spending with a new bank. As a COMER litigant wrote in their newsletter, "During the recent federal election, Trudeau floated an interesting plank about creating an infrastructure bank. My first response was 'You already have one. The Bank of Canada.' My second question was, 'Public or private?' Again we see both the colossal ignorance and deliberate obfuscation of money issues in this country by our leadership."[4]

A Liberal Party Backgrounder explained, "We will establish the Canada Infrastructure Bank (CIB) to provide low-cost financing to build new infrastructure projects. This new CIB will work in partnership with other orders of governments and Canada's financial community, so that the federal government can use its strong credit rating and lending authority to make it easier – and more affordable – for municipalities to finance the broad range of infrastructure projects their communities need ... Canada has become a global leader in infrastructure financing and we will work with the private sector and pools of capital that choose for themselves to invest in infrastructure projects."[5]

It's those "pools of capital" – including Wall Street titans like Goldman Sachs – that are set to profit handsomely from Canada's new infrastructure lending and spending spree.

In a cynical move, the Liberal Backgrounder didn't mention the interest-free loans of the past, but it did cite their results in order to tout the Liberal Party's "transformative investment plan" for Canada: "A large part of Canada's 20th century prosperity was made possible by nation-building projects – projects that without leadership from the government of Canada would not have been possible ... the St. Lawrence Seaway served as a foundation for prosperity in Quebec and Ontario; the Trans-Canada Highway links Canadians from coast to coast; and our electricity projects, pipelines, airports and canals have made it possible to develop our natural resources, power our cities, and connect with each other and the world."[6]

Pools of Capital

Enthused about Justin Trudeau's victory and his infrastructure campaign platform, Paul Krugman wrote in the *New York Times* (October 23, 2015), "We're living in a world awash with savings that the private sector doesn't want to invest and is eager to lend to governments at very low interest rates. It's obviously a good idea to borrow at those low, low rates ... Let's hope then, that Mr. Trudeau stays with the program. He has an opportunity to show the world what truly responsible fiscal policy looks like."[7]

Of course, borrowing from the Bank of Canada at NO interest rates would be even more fiscally responsible, and would keep policy decisions out of the hands of foreign lenders.

2. The Rise of the Overlords

The "father" of the Bank of Canada was a brilliant statesman and Member of Parliament from British Columbia named Gerald Gratton McGeer. In the midst of the Great Depression, McGeer analyzed the economic structure and wrote a 1935 report called "The Conquest of Poverty," in which he exposed some "great fallacies" operating at the time.

He wrote: "The proposition that there was safety in [private] banker management of the monetary system, and the theory that governments could not, to the advantage of the general community, issue national currency and credit, free of interest charge for the purpose of financing public enterprise are now openly in question. Once these great fallacies are recognized, the public will soon demand that government take over the credit machinery and provide the purchasing power of exchange necessary to finance progress."[1]

The Prime Minister of Canada at the time, William Lyon MacKenzie King, echoed McGeer's views on needed monetary reform. He told the public in an August 1935 radio address: "Once a nation parts with control of its currency and credit, it matters not who makes that nation's laws. Usury, once in control, will wreck any nation. Until the control of the issue of currency and credit is restored to government and recognized as its most conspicuous and sacred responsibility, all talk of the sovereignty of Parliament and of democracy is idle and futile."[2]

The stage was set for the creation of the Bank of Canada (BOC) in 1935, and its nationalization in 1938, with the federal government purchasing all the privately-held shares. What followed was a remarkable transformation of the country through interest-free BOC loans from 1938 until 1974, and as Bill Abram (now deceased) noted, "no great national debt was created."[3] When a loan was provided by the BOC to the federal or provincial government, it was repaid directly back to the publicly-owned BOC.

Canada was able to finance its participation in World War II, its transformation from a mostly rural to an industrialized country, its creation of virtually full employment, and its postwar rise in the standard of living – financing postsecondary education, health care, social safety nets, etc. – through the BOC without causing inflationary problems or borrowing from private lenders.

Given this achievement, why did the Liberal government of Pierre Trudeau abandon this path in 1974?

Rise of the Overlords

In his book *The Money Mafia*, Paul Hellyer writes that the system "worked splendidly for 35 years until 1974, when the Bank of Canada unilaterally changed the rules. As far as I know – and I and others have spent many hours in research without finding any evidence that would refute it – this was done without either advising or obtaining the consent of the Canadian government that owns 100% of the [BOC] shares on behalf of Canadian taxpayers. The Governor of the Bank of Canada, Gerald K. Bouey, simply announced [in 1974] that the Bank was adopting monetarism. There was no mention that this was being done to conform to a policy of the BIS [Bank for International Settlements] in Basel, Switzerland. Of much greater significance was the failure to disclose that the Bank was adopting the BIS' prohibition of providing low cost money to governments. In future, we would have to borrow in the market, and pay market [interest] rates."[4]

1974 was also the year that the U.S. lifted capital controls, allowing the cross-border movements of capital by which U.S. private banks became the centre of international finance.[5]

In a July 2016 email, Hellyer told me that Gerald Bouey simply gave a speech in Western Canada in which "he advised the public that the Bank was forthwith adopting monetarism – a theory proposed by Nobel Laureate Milton Friedman and his colleagues at the University of Chicago."

The monetary theory emanating from "the Chicago School" of economics at the University of Chicago – sometimes known as neoliberalism, "trickle-down economics," or "free market" capitalism – was sweeping the economic world in the 1970s, perhaps best known to most by England's Margaret Thatcher, who set out to privatize everything.

Right-wing economists such as Friedrich Hayek, Milton Friedman and their acolytes believed that "free markets" are efficient, rational and fair, and should be self-regulating with no government interference. This neoliberal economic policy aimed for unregulated (liberalized) "free markets," reduced government and regulation, cutbacks to social programs, union-busting, mass privatization of state assets, and free trade.

Naomi Klein's 2008 best-seller *The Shock Doctrine: The Rise of Disaster Capitalism* provides the best history of the "Chicago Boys" in action, starting with the 1973 overthrow of Salvador Allende in Chile and Pinochet's adoption of Friedman's economic model, which spread (along with corporate and state terror) to Argentina in 1976 and then throughout Latin America's Southern Cone.[6]

Before he was killed by the Argentina junta, journalist Rodolfo Walsh called the economic model imposed on his country "planned misery," throwing tens of millions of people into extreme poverty virtually overnight.[7] Economist Michel Chossudovsky, who was teaching in Chile in 1973, has written, "From one day to the next, an entire country was precipitated into abysmal poverty," and in less than a year, "eighty-five per cent of the Chilean population had been driven below the poverty line."[8] Chossudovsky saw the same "Chicago School" model imposed "in country after country." His 1997 book, *The Globalization of Poverty and the New World Order*, was one of the first to expose the workings of Friedman's economic model.[9]

This was the planned destruction of a nation's economy in order to replace it with the "free market" desired by multinational corporations and finance capital: creating a small class of overlords and a vastly impoverished underclass.

As Murray Dobbin wrote, during the 1970s "... international finance got its chance to launch the free market counter-revolution" by adopting "Milton Friedman's radical free market ideas: putting the creation of credit into private hands and creating debt burdens [for nations] which would restrict the potential for democratic governance ... [Friedman's] ideology was shared by the Bank for International Settlements."[10]

Escalating Debt

In Canada, the effect of BOC Governor Gerald Bouey's decision to adopt the Milton Friedman model dictated by the BIS was dramatic and almost immediate. Bill Abrams published a chart (based on StatsCan data) showing that from 1940 to 1974, Canada's national debt remained very low (well under $30 billion), but after 1974, when all levels of government were forced to borrow from private lenders, Canada's national debt skyrocketed – the chart shows almost a 90-degree angle in the rise – to $523 billion in 2005.[11] This escalating debt has been used ever since to justify cuts to Canada's health care and social programs, from the Mulroney era on into the present.

As Hellyer told me, in 2016 the national debt is $615 billion and is "headed to more than $700 billion by the end of the four year mandate of the present [Justin Trudeau] government. Even more astounding, harried taxpayers have had to pay more than $1.1 trillion in interest in that period" from 1974 to 2015.

Obviously, Bouey's decision meant tremendous profits for the banks, which were similarly reaping vast compound interest payments from other governments that followed the Friedman gospel and bowed to the dictates of the Bank for International Settlements.

Blaming Trudeau?

Hellyer told me, "When they hear these numbers, many people

blame Pierre Trudeau who was prime minister when the change of policy occurred. I suspected that this was an unfair assumption. So I got permission to look at the former prime minister's private papers for the period in question. There was not a word indicating that he had been consulted by Governor Bouey, or that he was in any way involved in the decision. He had been informed about the adoption of 'monetarism' but there was not even a hint that the Bank of Canada was arbitrarily changing the system," which gave private banks a monopoly on the creation of money in Canada.

"To double-check that I hadn't missed anything," Hellyer told me, "I phoned Dr. John English, Pierre Trudeau's official biographer, who had unlimited access to all his papers, and asked if he or any of his research team had seen anything that indicated the prime minister had been in the loop. The answer was 'no,' 'nothing'."

Hellyer maintains that the "bottom line is that the Governor of the Bank of Canada [Gerald Bouey] unilaterally, and without authority, made a decision that has cost the Canadian people more than a trillion dollars in interest, and left them with a debt that can never be repaid."

But not everyone lets Pierre Trudeau off the hook. Just because there's no paper trail doesn't necessarily mean that there were no private conversations or phone calls between the two men. Perhaps we'll never know for sure whether Gerald Bouey's 1974 decision was unilateral, but we can place it in the historical context of Milton Friedman's economic model and see the results. We can also place it in the context of the rise of the BIS.

"Money Funnel"

The Bank for International Settlements has been called "the secret bank that runs the world." Established in 1930 through intergovernmental agreements by about a dozen countries, its original purpose was to facilitate reparations payments imposed on Germany by the Treaty of Versailles after World War I. But as Charles Higham revealed in *Trading with the Enemy*, the BIS soon turned out to be "a money funnel for American and British funds to flow into Hitler's coffers and to help Hitler build up his war machine."[12]

Higham's book and Adam Lebor's *Tower of Basel* provide the frightening history of the BIS – a bank which now functions as an "unelected, unaccountable and secretive financial institution" that issues "policy prescriptions for democratic governments."[13]

Lebor calls the BIS "the world's most exclusive club," whose 18 members gather six times a year to attend the Economic Consultative Committee (ECC), where they deliberate in the utmost secrecy and make decisions that affect every nation's economy. As the bank for central banks (many now privatized), the BIS's members include central bank governors from around the world.

"In theory," Lebor wrote in 2013, "sensible housekeeping and mutual cooperation, overseen by the BIS, will keep the global financial system functioning smoothly. In theory. The reality is that we have moved beyond recession into a deep structural crisis, one fueled by the [private] banks' greed and rapacity, which threatens all of our financial security."[14] The BIS is at the top of a global network of money, power, and covert global influence.

Georgetown University professor Carrol Quigley wrote in 1964, "The powers of financial capitalism had another far-reaching aim, nothing less than to create a world system of financial control in private hands able to dominate the political system of each country and the economy of the world as a whole. This system was to be controlled in a feudalist fashion by the central banks of the world acting in concert, by secret agreements arrived at in frequent private meetings and conferences. The apex of the system was to be the Bank for International Settlements in Basel, Switzerland."[15]

The BIS is essentially a sovereign state which pays no taxes, whose grounds and offices are sovereign territory, whose annual meetings are secret, and whose personnel have diplomatic immunity. "No government has legal jurisdiction over the bank, nor do any governments have oversight over its operations."[16]

Paul Hellyer has noted that after World War II the influence of the BIS "became all pervasive. It played a significant role in the unification of Europe. Most important of all, just as the top bankers had hoped, it became a powerful vehicle for the transfer of power from democratic nation states to an unelected, unaccountable, bureaucratic institution acting on the private advice from the world's top bankers."[17]

When Gerald Bouey bowed to the BIS's dictates, the publicly-owned Bank of Canada arguably lost its independence, with its policy-making on monetary issues effectively transferred to the private and foreign-based financial industry. The fact that this was also happening to other countries at the time is, of course, no consolation.

That crucial decision in 1974 coincided with another important phenomenon.

The Debt Trap

John Perkins' 2004 book *Confessions of an Economic Hit Man* shocked readers into realizing just how finance capital had indebted and terrorized the Third World since the late 1960s. Perkins described a system by which consultants like himself were sent to Third World governments to convince their leaders to take on huge debts for building massive infrastructure projects. While the loans came from the World Bank, the IMF, US Agency for International Development (USAID) and other lending institutions overseen by the BIS, the money went directly to the big engineering, construction and consulting companies: Bechtel, Stone & Webster, Brown & Root, Chas T. Main, Halliburton, General Electric, and others. Perkins admits that he and other economic hit men cheated countries around the globe out of trillions of dollars in order to enrich U.S. corporations.[18]

Chillingly, Perkins revealed that governments which refused to indebt their countries (for infrastructure projects that usually only benefitted an elite few) were then targeted by "the jackals," assassins who killed the leaders; and if that didn't work to force a "regime change," the U.S. military would invade the country. This fusion of finance capital and military power has rarely been so clearly explained from the inside. Moreover, once a Third World government had been saddled with massive debt, it could be further manipulated and exploited for political purposes.

This was the "big project paradigm" for development, aligned with Milton Friedman's economic model, that took hold in the 1970s and was virtually forced onto poor countries, preventing their governments from devoting funds to poverty reduction, land reform, social services, import substitution (i.e., local production and manufacturing), and other measures that would benefit their own populations.

The "Chicago Boys"

By comparison, the BIS' insistence that Canada (and other developed countries) abandon their government lending was not as draconian, but it fit the pattern: removing monetary sovereignty, imposing a debt burden, requiring restrictions on deficit spending, curtailing funding for social programs, and limiting government power – all leading to the goals of Milton Friedman and the Chicago School: "free markets," reduced government and regulation, austerity budgets, mass privatization, and free trade.

The Chicago School inspired a neoliberal "Calgary school" of thought, thoroughly documented in Donald Gutstein's 2014 book *Harperism*. Gutstein also provides an explanation of the confusing term "neoliberalism," which has nothing to do with "liberal" thinking but instead is about liberalizing markets and trade. He writes that this ideology "is properly called neo-liberalism because, in contrast to libertarians who want a small, powerless state that leaves people alone, neo-liberals require a strong state that uses its power to create and enforce markets, and prop them up when they fail, as happened after the 2007-08 financial meltdown."[19]

Along with the creation of the right-wing Fraser Institute in 1974 (which lists the deceased Friedrich Hayek on its board), much of Canada – and not just BOC Governor Gerald Bouey – was falling in line with neoliberalism.

Author Greg Palast studied economics with "the Chicago Boys" under Friedman, and in his book *Vulture's Picnic*, he notes: "The quickest of the Chicago students, often armed with mighty computer algorithms that could make Einstein sweat, praised Friedman and the free market to the sky – and made billions proving Friedman wrong." Contrary to Friedman's claim that "free markets" are fair and self-regulating, the Chicago Boys showed that "[t]he market could be fixed, fondled, fucked with, bent, and the suckers kept deaf, dumb and blind, have their pockets slashed, lose their jobs, homes and pensions to the arbs [arbitrators], the hedge fund operators, and Enron traders guided by their secret, well-proven theorem: Milton Friedman doesn't know his ass from his elbow about economics."[20]

The folks at COMER (founded in 1988) could see that Milton Friedman's acolytes (including those at the BIS) were taking the world in a dangerous direction, although they tended to be more polite about it than Palast. COMER co-founder William Krehm wrote in 1993: "The BIS grew in power as its dogma gained control of, among other organizations, the International Monetary Fund and the World Bank... [which] have forced the citizens of nations short on trousers to tighten their belts," while the money lent to them "ended up in secret numbered accounts, held by accommodating banks."[21]

Back to the Future

Unlike other developed countries in the G7, Canada still has a publicly-owned central bank. That is why COMER launched its lawsuit: it is still possible to return the Bank of Canada to its original mandate.

COMER's Herb Wiseman told me by email how the transition could work: "Debt from the federal government is in treasury bills and bonds. They all have time limits or maturation dates. When the dates come due, all the Bank of Canada has to do is purchase them itself. As well, the BOC can create a deposit in the government's account and that cash can be used to fund infrastructure. Paul Hellyer has another plan that would also work [*www.canadianbankreformers.ca*]."

The newly elected government of Justin Trudeau, however, seems intent on bypassing the COMER lawsuit and instituting an entirely different bank for building infrastructure – one that will further indebt the country.[22] As well, with their interest in something called "asset recycling," the Liberal government is embarking on a terrible irony, historically speaking. Gerald Gratton McGeer wrote in his 1935 report that the private banking systems' control of money-creation must be wiped out "in much the same way, and for the same reason that we wiped out toll gates and private management of public roads and highways" in the nineteenth century.[23] As we shall see, the financial sector (with the help of governments) intends to turn the clock way back.

That too has long been part of the Milton Friedman economic model. The Chicago School "wanted to expropriate what workers and governments had built during those decades of frenetic public works ... As far as Friedman was concerned, all this shared wealth should be transferred into private hands, on principle."[24]

3. A 21ˢᵗ Century Trojan Horse

In the spring of 2016, a rumour started spreading that the COMER lawsuit was now defunct. The Press For Truth (PFT) website posted a piece on February 25 entitled "COMER Case Against Bank of Canada Reaches its End," following a February 8ᵗʰ Federal Court ruling by Justice James Russell. PFT claimed that the case had been "tossed out of court and there isn't any more opportunity for them [COMER]" to go forward with the lawsuit.[1]

Before penning this premature obituary, PFT apparently did not contact COMER or lawyer Rocco Galati, who on March 3, 2016 filed an appeal to the Federal Court of Appeal and stated that Justice Russell had "inexplicably reversed himself" and "blatantly erred," and "If redress is not had at the Federal Court of Appeal, COMER is committed to then taking the case to the Supreme Court of Canada."[2]

Obviously, the lawsuit is alive and kicking.

In August 2016, COMER's Herb Wiseman told me, "We are back in court in the fall appealing the decision where Justice Russell overturned himself and a higher court. The last information on our website is still current."

Meanwhile, the powers-that-be seem intent on confusing Canadians.

Who's the Boss?

In mid-April 2016, Bank of Canada (BOC) Governor Stephen Poloz surprised many when he stated that the Federal Finance Minister "is not my boss," while insisting that the Bank of Canada "is a fully independent policymaker."

In reporting this, the *Financial Post* (April 13, 2016) also quoted a UK-based economist who said, "Technically, the bank is a Crown corporation and the shares are owned by the Minister of Finance. So as the main shareholder, it could force some decision ... But in real life, central banks have fought for their independence, which is widely recognized as sound policy and means that the finance minister does not interfere in the bank's affairs and allows the bank to be independent."[3]

But according to members of COMER, the *Bank of Canada Act* is clear about just who is Poloz's "boss." Article 14:2 of the *Act* states that in any difference of opinion between the Governor and the Finance Minister regarding monetary policy, the Minister may "give to the Governor a written directive ... and the Bank shall comply with that directive," which would then have to be published in the *Canada Gazette* and presented to Parliament.

COMER Chair Ann Emmett told me during a phone interview that Poloz's statement is apparently based in the belief or theory that there should be an arms-length relationship between the BOC and the federal government, but "that doesn't mean the Bank of Canada is fully independent." Moreover, the BOC "isn't like other central banks" because the Bank of Canada is "still a publicly-owned bank," Emmett said, and the sole shareholder is actually the people of Canada.

In what appears to be a way to side-step the COMER lawsuit and the Bank of Canada, (and the *Bank of Canada Act?*), the Liberal government of Justin Trudeau is moving forward with its plan – vaguely mentioned during the 2015 election campaign – for a new Canada Infrastructure Bank (CIB) to arrange financing for $120 billion in infrastructure spending over the next ten years. The CIB would apparently be the middleman between private investors and local governments (municipal and provincial) looking to fund infrastructure. A Canadian legal magazine has reported that the CIB would "assist municipalities with funding and financing, working with the financial community to provide low-cost financing, including loan guarantees."[4]

While the Trudeau government hasn't said whether the CIB would be a Crown corporation, some important details have emerged.

The Advisors

Just before the March 2016 release of the Federal Budget (which didn't directly mention the CIB), the *Ottawa Citizen*'s Jason Fekete reported: "Ottawa has already taken steps to move the CIB project forward. It has recruited a Canadian investment banker working at Bank of America Merrill Lynch in the U.S. to help design the CIB and advise Infrastructure Minister Amarjeet Sohi on the project."[5]

Working voluntarily out of Sohi's office until late September, this Bank of America Merrill Lynch banker "will also work with large pension funds in Canada as part of the Liberal government's efforts to persuade them to invest in Canadian infrastructure such as transit projects." Fekete added that "the government has also created a new, executive group position of Chief, Infrastructure at Finance Canada to advise Finance Minister Bill Morneau on the development of the Infrastructure Bank, the plans and priorities of the Infrastructure minister, and the Finance Department's relationship with PPP Canada, a Crown corporation that delivers public infrastructure through public-private partnerships (P3s)."

As far as I can determine, the identity of the Bank of America Merrill Lynch banker advising Sohi has not been revealed as of September 2016. Sohi's office did not respond to my request for information.

Merrill Lynch and the Bank of America (which merged in 2008) were both involved in the massive Wall Street mishandling of asset-backed securities and investments that led to the 2008 Great Recession and the bank bailouts – which shook the world's financial stability, with repercussions that have continued ever since.

It's been reported that "backdoor bailouts" for Merrill Lynch and Bank of America reached "a combined $11.5 billion" in taxpayer monies.[6] Those "backdoor bailouts" were only a fraction of the money given to those two banks during the aftermath of the Wall Street crash. The *Rolling Stone*'s Matt Taibbi, in a scathing 2012 article, says that Bank of

America received at least $45 billion from taxpayers, even though it "has systematically ripped off almost everyone with whom it has a significant business relationship, cheating investors, insurers, depositors, homeowners, shareholders, pensioners and taxpayers."[7]

So why would the Trudeau government choose someone from Bank of America Merrill Lynch to advise them on setting up a CIB?

One possible answer comes if we look at the single biggest shareholder in Bank of America – a little-known company called BlackRock.[8]

World's Biggest Investor

According to *The Economist* (Dec. 7, 2013), this company (that nobody has heard of) turns out to be the world's biggest investor, with more than $4 trillion in assets under management, and another $15 trillion that it manages (under something called the Aladdin risk-management platform) for investors worldwide.[9]

So influential is BlackRock that, according to *The Economist*, the company advised governments in the U.S., Greece and Britain on what to do with toxic assets from crashing banks, with co-founder, chair and CEO Larry Fink becoming a Washington insider.[10]

These governments sought Fink's advice, despite the fact that (as *Fortune* reported in 2008) BlackRock's Larry Fink "was an early and vigorous promoter [of] the same mortgage-backed securities" responsible for the crisis. "Now his firm is making millions cleaning up these toxic assets," *Fortune* noted.[11]

Besides being Bank of America's biggest shareholder, BlackRock owns part of Merrill Lynch and in 2009 BlackRock snapped up Barclays' asset-management business, thereby boosting the assets under its control well into the trillions.

The current Board of Directors for BlackRock (blackrock.com) has some interesting people and corporate connections, including one Canadian – Gordon Nixon, the former President and CEO of the Royal Bank of Canada who retired in 2014 and was appointed to the BlackRock Board in July 2015.[12]

In its extensive 2013 coverage of BlackRock, *The Economist* focused on the company's risk-management platform called Aladdin – a massive data centre that "single-handedly manages almost as much money as all the world's private equity and hedge funds," while advising more than 100 major investors worldwide on where and how to invest.[13] Calling Aladdin's "prognostications" somewhat "discomfiting," *The Economist* noted: "Buyers, sellers and regulators may all be relying on the same assumptions, simply because they are all consulting Aladdin. In a panic, this could increase the risk of all of them wanting to jump the same way, making things worse."[14]

With BlackRock advising on $15 trillion worth of investments globally, it wasn't just *The Economist* that was worried. As the *Wall Street Journal* reported, the U.S. Treasury Department's Office of Financial Research issued a 2013 report which "concluded that asset-management firms [like BlackRock] and the funds they run were 'vulnerable to shocks' and may engage in 'herding' behaviour that could amplify a shock to the financial system."[15]

But BlackRock lobbied hard against such a view, and in April 2016 avoided greater oversight from regulators in the U.S.[16]

"Herding" Behaviour

Regardless of just who has been doing the "herding," it's obvious that, over the past two decades and increasingly since 2008, big investors like Bank of America, JP Morgan Chase, Goldman Sachs, and Morgan Stanley have been buying up and gaining control over what's known as "the real economy" – the already-built airports, roads, sea ports, electricity production and transmission systems, water and wastewater systems, utilities, etc., across much of the developed world. These investments provide shareholders with increasing long-term, steady profits from tolls and rents that previously went to the public owners of the infrastructure.

As *Web of Debt* author Ellen Brown warned in 2013, such a trend represents "a return to a feudal landlord economy of unearned profits from rent-seeking."[17]

The *Toronto Star* explained that such investments are "low-risk" and "with a predictable, long-term return" for the investor, which is why the Canadian Pension Plan Investment Board (CPPIB) – the investment arm of the CPP – in 2015 bought "a one-third stake in Associated British

Ports, which owns 21 ports in the UK, for $2.4 billion," and a 25% stake ($500 million) in one road in Sydney, Australia.[18]

Mark Wiseman, the CEO of the CPPIB (with $283 billion in assets), recently told Bloomberg News that the CPPIB is looking for "projects of scale" – airports, roads, ports, etc. "Canada Pension, like many other large global investors, would rather acquire mature infrastructure assets than finance new projects because they're safer, Wiseman said. He encouraged the [Canadian] federal government to look to places like Australia or the UK as examples of how Ottawa could utilize the capital of these global funds to meet its own infrastructure needs."[19]

The Australian Model

In 2013, the right-wing Australian government established its "Asset Recycling Initiative" – a program by which states and territorial governments decide which infrastructure assets to sell to the private sector, while the federal government grants 15 per cent of the sale price to the states/territories. The federal funds and proceeds from the sales are then used to fund new infrastructure projects.[20]

Australian critics of "asset recycling" say it is basically "selling a hospital to build a road," with the federal government bribing local governments with incentive payments in order to sell off public assets.[21]

Canada's CUPE (Canadian Union of Public Employees) calls "asset recycling" basically "a new way to privatize all or part of a public asset such as a hydro utility or a government building" by selling or borrowing against physical assets to generate money for new investment. The Ontario government of Kathleen Wynne is engaging in "asset recycling" by selling off a majority stake in Hydro One (the electricity transmission/distribution system) in order to finance public transit – selling off transmission lines in order to pay for transit lines – thereby "sacrificing billions of dollars in future revenues from the crown corporation for a one-time payment."[22]

The Royal Bank of Canada and the Bank of Nova Scotia acted as underwriters in Hydro One's initial sell-off of 81.1 million shares in November 2015, with both banks holding an "option to purchase an additional 8.15 million shares."[23]

The C.D. Howe Institute is recommending that other local governments in Canada imitate what Ontario is doing.

In its January 2016 brief about infrastructure financing, the think tank stated, "Canadian cities should first look to emulate Ontario's provincial policy of selling underutilized assets – such as electricity distribution companies – to generate funding for infrastructure that governments necessarily must own."[24] (Not everyone considers electricity distribution systems to be an "underutilized asset." In 2014, Warren Buffett snapped up AltaLink in Alberta for a mere $3.2 billion, after taxpayers had poured $16 billion into building the electricity transmission infrastructure serving four-fifths of the province.)[25]

Although the Trudeau Liberals' March 2016 budget did not mention an infrastructure bank, it did refer to "asset recycling" in one sentence: "Where it is in the public interest, engage public pension plans and other innovative sources of funding – such as demand management initiatives and asset recycling – to increase the long-term affordability and sustainability of infrastructure in Canada."

As first reported by the Canadian Press's Andy Blatchford, "The federal government has identified a potential source of cash to help pay for Canada's mounting infrastructure costs – and it could involve leasing or selling stakes in major public assets such as highways, rail lines, and ports. A line [mentioning asset recycling] tucked into last month's federal budget reveals the Liberals are considering making public assets available to non-government investors, like public pension funds ... Asset recycling is gaining an increasing amount of international attention and one of the best-known, large-scale examples is found in Australia."[26]

Blatchford further reported: "Australia's asset recycling model has been praised by influential Canadians such as Mark Wiseman, president and CEO of the Canadian Pension Plan Investment Board (CPPIB). 'With growing infrastructure deficits worldwide ... we often reference this model with our own government and others as one to follow to incent and attract long-term capital,' Wiseman said in prepared remarks of a September speech [entitled "Building the Case for a Long-Term Perspective"] in Sydney to the Canadian Australian Chamber of Commerce."[27]

Tangled Web

In her series about the CPP and the CPPIB published by the *Huffington Post* in January 2013, Amy MacPherson revealed the "dramatic changes" made to the CPP by the Stephen Harper government when first elected.

MacPherson wrote: "In 2007, new legislation altered CPP practices through measures contained in Bill C-36. By April 2007, all CPP assets were transferred to control of the investment board ... and in 2012 they changed from passive management to active management techniques. Aggressive trading requires a team of involved experts, and staff at the CPP ballooned from 70 to 811 in the same short period. They've opened offices in Hong Kong and London, took on riskier markets, decreased Canadian equities in favour of foreign projects, hedged currency and shifted public holdings to private interests."[28]

Overseeing the CPPIB's "active management techniques" is a high-powered board of directors that includes Heather Munroe-Blum (director of the C. D. Howe Institute and the Royal Bank of Canada, and a member of the Trilateral Commission), Douglas W. Mahaffy (former managing director and head of Investment Banking Ontario, of Merrill Lynch Canada Inc.) and Kathleen Taylor (chair of the Royal Bank of Canada).

With two Royal Bank of Canada directors on the CPPIB, this brings us back to Gordon Nixon, the former head of the Royal Bank of Canada and now a board member of Larry Fink's BlackRock – the top shareholder in Bank of America Merrill Lynch and also the world's largest investment company, which may have been "herding" investors in worrying ways.

As it turns out, BlackRock's Larry Fink is also involved with CPPIB's Mark Wiseman in a venture called Focusing Capital on the Long Term (FCLT), apparently a think tank with both men on the Advisory Board. The mission statement (*fclt.org*) reads: "In 2013, CPPIB and McKinsey & Company co-founded Focusing Capital on the Long Term to develop practical structures, metrics, and approaches for longer-term behaviours in the investment and business worlds."

In addition to the ten advisory members in FCLT, there are 12 members – most of them people who oversee pension funds and sovereign wealth funds, including Michael Sabia, President and CEO of the Caisse de depot et placement du Quebec, and Wayne Kozun of the Ontario Teachers' Pension Plan.

So the Canada Pension Plan Investment Board, the Caisse de depot et placement du Quebec, and the Ontario Teachers' Pension Plan are directly involved with Larry Fink, co-founder and CEO of BlackRock, the biggest shareholder in Bank of America Merrill Lynch.

This may seem to be a tangled web, but arguably now we know better why the Canadian federal government has asked a Bank of America Merrill Lynch banker to advise on the proposed Canada Infrastructure Bank.

PR Firms' Involvement

In the globalized economy, giant investors expect to be able to pry open and seize the public assets of any country, including those in the developed world. Moreover, "asset recycling" sounds so much nicer than "structural adjustment program."

According to speaking notes, CPPIB's Mark Wiseman told the Canadian Australian Chamber of Commerce in September 2015, "We have almost A$7 billion invested here in Australia, or about A$1.5 billion more than the last time I spoke here" in 2013.[29]

Most Canadians don't know it, but Canada's public pension funds are often criticized outside the country for helping to privatize public assets. CUPE Researcher Kevin Skerrett recently wrote, "Workers' pension funds must not become tools for privatization, whether in Canada or around the world. At the November 2015 National Convention, CUPE delegates overwhelmingly approved a policy resolution that committed the union to opposing 'the use of public pension funds for privatization'."[30]

By 2012, Reuters was calling Canadian public pension funds "stealth investors" flying "under the radar," having bought up "London's Heathrow Airport, toll roads in Chile, real estate from Manhattan to São Paulo, gas pipelines in the United States, water treatment plants in Britain, timberlands in Australia."[31]

The "asset recycling" concept has first been applied in Australia, and it looks like the same team is hoping to apply it across Canada, and possibly the U.S.

As well, a major PR firm appears to be involved in the effort. One of the Members of the FCLT think tank is Richard Edelman, President and CEO of Edelman – one of the world's largest PR firms, with 67 offices worldwide. (This is the same PR firm that was let go by TransCanada Corporation in 2014 after leaked documents revealed shady tactics for dealing with opposition to the Energy East tarsands pipeline.)[32] An Edelman office is the media-contact for inquiries about FCLT.

In addition, CPPIB director Michael Goldberg is also a director of B.C.-based Resource Works, which (according to its website) promotes "fact-based dialogue on responsible resource development in British Columbia." Critics say Resource Works is a collection of PR flacks working especially for the oil and gas industry.[33]

Resource Works is currently promoting the export of Site C dam-generated electricity (scheduled to be online as of 2024) to power tar sands development in Alberta, enabling (as their website puts it) the "expansion of the oil sands powered by clean energy to avoid climate change." The B.C. Christy Clark government (which has ties to Resource Works) is lobbying for federal "green infrastructure" cash to build this grid to Alberta, while the two provinces are discussing the possibility of a pipeline-for-electricity swap, in which Alberta would agree to buy B.C. electricity in exchange for B.C.'s permission for a tar sands export pipeline – Kinder Morgan's proposed Trans Mountain expansion and/or Enbridge's Northern Gateway – to the West Coast.[34]

As reported in 2013, BlackRock is the biggest shareholder in ExxonMobil (majority owner of Imperial Oil) and Shell Oil[35], two of the tarsands producers pushing for pipeline access to tidewater on Canada's coasts.

Struggling Local Governments

Provinces and municipalities across Canada are struggling financially, as neoliberal federal governments since the mid-1990s have cut transfer payments and further downloaded costs onto local governments (which have the least ability to raise revenues, basically through property taxes and user fees).

As Council of Canadians' Maude Barlow and Paul Moist (national president of the Canadian Union of Public Employees) wrote in 2012, "The federal strategy appears to be to starve municipalities of infrastructure cash until they are forced to privatize through a P3," despite evidence "from auditors' general reports across Canada that P3s are often more costly and less efficient than fully public models."[36]

In 2014, B.C.'s Auditor General revealed that the provincial government is paying nearly twice as much to borrow through P3 private financing than if it borrowed the money itself. As CUPE noted, "Over the average 35 year lifespan of P3 contracts, this means the [B.C.] government is paying more than $2 billion more just in private financing."[37]

In December 2014, Ontario's Auditor General Bonnie Lysyk blasted the Liberals' use of private money to finance new hospitals and transit, revealing that Infrastructure Ontario's use of P3s had cost $8 billion more taxpayer dollars than traditional public financing would have.[38]

The use of P3s in the United Kingdom led to what has been called "a full-blown fiscal crisis," with governments indebted to banks and corporations for 222 billion pounds sterling in order to pay for P3 projects valued at 56.5 billion pounds – an astonishing rip-off of taxpayers. UK's "Private Finance Initiative," in place since the 1990s, was the forerunner to the Canadian P3 program, but no one bothered to explain to Canadians just what happened to the UK through its use of P3 private financing.[39]

More recently, Auditor General Bonnie Lysyk revealed Ontario's mismanagement of the electricity system through vastly overpaying IPPs (independent power producers). The Auditor General determined that because of the terms for this partial privatization of electricity production, between 2008 and 2014 Ontarians overpaid for electricity by as much as $37 billion.[40] The biggest IPP in Ontario is TransCanada Corp.; others include Bruce Power, TransAlta, NextEra, and Enbridge. The long-term contracts with these IPPs mean that Ontarians will be overpaying by billions of dollars for electricity for many years.

Similarly in B.C., taxpayers have a $50 billion secondary debt burden under IPP contracts, according to retired economist Erik Andersen, and they are paying "exorbitant premiums" because of this partial privatization of BC Hydro. [41]

So with P3s and partial privatizations now considered somewhat "toxic" by much of the taxpaying public, it appears that a new euphemism of "asset recycling" has been created, along with a new strategy of selling off assets in order to build new ones. Conveniently, all this is happening at the same time that rates for borrowing from private lenders are low.

The growing hype about "asset recycling" might well appeal to politicians, unless the public catches on and understands what's happening. Pension managers team up with private investors to take stakes in big assets, such as Australia's Port of Melbourne – the country's largest container terminal and the so-called "jewel in the crown" – which the government is hoping will sell/lease for $6 billion in order to finance other infrastructure. [42]

In late September 2016, the deal for the Port of Melbourne was signed for $7.3 billion, with the Ontario Municipal Employees Retirement System (OMERS) taking one fifth ownership, along with China Investment Corp and several others. [43]

Needlessly starved for capital, governments are doing everything but take back their own monetary powers.

Hidden History

For decades (1938 to 1974), the publicly-owned Bank of Canada funded a wide range of public infrastructure projects by providing near-zero interest loans to federal and provincial governments, without causing inflationary problems or debt to private and foreign lenders. [44] That hidden history is now emerging, thanks to the efforts of many.

By contrast, the proposed Canada Infrastructure Bank looks like a Trojan Horse that could usher in more indebtedness and more corporate control – as neofeudal landlords – over major infrastructure such as water and wastewater systems, electricity systems, airports, ports, etc.

The founding members of COMER have long questioned neoliberalism's economic model based on exponential growth, with escalating private profits considered supreme. As COMER Vice-chair Herb Wiseman told me by email, "P3s are not really about government financing because of scarce money, but another con job by the corporations to expand their operations in order to enhance shareholder value. It is made to look like governments are asking for this form of help when in fact it serves the corporate interests for never-ending growth on a finite planet."

Globe & Mail columnist Konrad Yakabuski has urged "sober second thought" about infrastructure spending, citing examples in Spain, Greece and Japan (seduced by low borrowing rates from private lenders) where massive spending has created "money pit" infrastructure that nobody uses.[45] Yakabuski noted, "If government spending on superlatively smooth highways, sleek subways and far-stretching fast trains was the ticket to success, Japan, Spain, and Greece would lead the global economy. Instead, infrastructure spending has been a major source of their debt-induced woes."[46] Yakabuski refers to "our infrastructure envy," suggesting that Canada is being herded down a path that other governments have already followed into further massive debt to private lenders.

Renowned economist Michael Hudson (author of *Killing the Host*) bluntly warns that this path is "the road to debt serfdom," with a rising financial oligarchy "impoverishing the 99%."[47]

The Trudeau government's appointment of a banker from Bank of America Merrill Lynch to advise on creating a new infrastructure bank is the most politicized appointment possible, aside from appointing Black-Rock's Larry Fink himself.

Meanwhile, on May 18, 2016 the *Financial Post* reported that Mark Wiseman, the chief executive of the Canada Pension Plan Investment Board, is leaving that post in June to take "a senior leadership role" at BlackRock in September 2016.[48]

4. The "New Economy Czar"

As of September 2016, the identity of that Bank of America Merrill Lynch banker appointed by Justin Trudeau to advise Canada on setting up a Canada Infrastructure Bank (CIB) still hadn't been divulged. What had become clear, however, is that the publicly-owned Bank of Canada (BOC) is quite cozy with Bank of America Merrill Lynch alumni passing through the revolving door that exists for bankers and their in-house economists.

On May 26, 2016, Reuters reported that the BOC had hired former Merrill Lynch economist Sheryl King as an advisor to represent the bank in its New York office, to "promote and strengthen ties between the Bank of Canada and New York's financial and economic communities, with an emphasis on financial market and financial stability developments."[1] Just why the BOC would need closer ties to Wall Street wasn't explained, nor did Reuters expand on why those stronger ties would have anything to do with "financial stability," given Wall Street's record.

Ms. King is reporting to Bank of Canada Deputy Governor Lynn Patterson – herself the former Canadian head of Bank of America Merrill Lynch, who became deputy governor at the BOC in 2014.[2]

Advisory Council

On May 14, 2016 Finance Minister Bill Morneau (former Chair of the C.D. Howe Institute) met for the first time with "his group of hand-picked advisers who will help the federal government create a plan to boost Canada's long-term growth."[3] Is this Advisory Council on Economic Growth the same thing as the "new, executive group position of Chief, Infrastructure" that Andy Blatchford reported on in March 2016? It sounds like it because their mid-May meeting was devoted to "exploring how the government can work together with institutional investors, such as public pension plans, to help pay for infrastructure projects, Morneau told CBC in an interview."[4]

The 14 Advisory Council members were reportedly joined at the meeting by four other key Cabinet ministers: Economic Development Minister Navdeep Bains, International Trade Minister Chrystia Freeland, Infrastructure Minister Amarjeet Sohi, and Labour Minister MaryAnn Mihvchuk.

With the Trudeau Liberals planning to spend $120 billion on infrastructure over the next ten years, Morneau told the CBC that he appointed Mark Wiseman (Canada Pension Plan Investment Board) and Michael Sabia (the Caisse de depot et placement du Quebec) to this Advisory Council on Economic Growth for specific reasons. "We can keep the money here [in Canada], it will help Canadian retirees, so we're thinking about, how can we amplify the federal investment by finding ways to work together with institutional investors? ... We're actively engaged in that discussion. That was a significant part of our day today because, as I said, we want to think about the long term and how we have the biggest impact – and they'll [Wiseman and Sabia] be part of that."[5]

But Mark Wiseman, as we know, announced just days after that meeting that he was moving on from the CPPIB to bigger and better things at Larry Fink's BlackRock.

Wiseman was appointed in late May as BlackRock's top executive overseeing its stock-picking operations; he was also appointed as a member of BlackRock's Global Executive Committee – an "exclusive club of fewer than two-dozen senior deputies to BlackRock Chief Executive Larry Fink and President Rob Kapito." Reuters further reported that

Wiseman "will also become chairman of Black Alternative Investors, a smaller, but highly-lucrative group of BlackRock investments, including its hedge funds and infrastructure business."[6]

"Highly lucrative" barely covers it, with BlackRock managing trillions of dollars. So now Mark Wiseman is well-positioned to advance BlackRock's infrastructure investment business in Canada and elsewhere.

By August 2016, the *Toronto Star* was reporting that Justin Trudeau had "spent part of the summer courting BlackRock, the world's largest investment manager, a $5-trillion juggernaut with its headquarters in New York City. Trudeau hopes some of that worldwide torrent of money can be diverted toward infrastructure projects in Canada."[7]

Focusing Capital

As we saw previously, Morneau's Advisory Council members Mark Wiseman and the Caisse's Michael Sabia have been working together with Larry Fink since 2013 at the think tank called Focusing Capital on the Long Term (FCLT). But there is another member of Morneau's Advisory Council on Economic Growth who is also an FCLT heavyweight; in fact, he is the Co-Chair with Wiseman of FCLT – but no one would know that unless they had accessed the FCLT website before early June 2016, by which time I noticed that all information about FCLT Co-Chairs, Advisors, and Members had been removed from the site.

The Chair of Morneau's Advisory Council on Economic Growth is Dominic Barton, who is Canada's so-called "New Economy Czar." The fact that Barton is also the Co-Chair of FCLT has not been divulged by the mainstream press, even though the government includes that fact on its website.

Barton is the global managing director of consulting giant McKinsey & Co. (which set up FCLT along with the Canada Pension Plan Investment Board). As Chair of Morneau's Advisory Council on Economic Growth, Barton's ideas reportedly include (in the reporter's words) "enticing huge investors from here and abroad to pour cash into major public infrastructure projects" and "boosting infrastructure investment in a big way – by finding cash in places outside the public treasury and even beyond Canadian borders."[8]

Indeed, Barton's ideas for infrastructure spending in Canada make the Trudeau Liberals' $120 billion look like thin medieval gruel. According to the Canadian Press, Barton "pegged the infrastructure gap – the difference between what Canada needs and what it has – at a level as high as $500 billion."[9]

It's an astonishing figure, suggesting that Barton believes Canadians' "infrastructure envy" can be pushed way past what the Trudeau Liberals have assumed. Indeed, Barton "believes Canada can lead the world" in infrastructure spending. He told CP's Andy Blatchford on May 20, 2016, "It's amazing that no G7 country has been investing in infrastructure when interest rates are at 50-year lows ... This is shocking."[10]

But it might be useful to ask: Who is Dominic Barton?

Canada's "New Economy Czar"

Barton has been the global managing director of McKinsey & Co. since 2009, having worked at the firm for decades. He's also a trustee of the Brookings Institution, on the board of the Asia Pacific Foundation of Canada, and a member of the advisory board of the Ecofiscal Commission in Canada.

Karl Nerenberg of *Rabble.ca* has called Dominic Barton "a truly global economic citizen," and that's certainly true.[11] According to Nerenberg, Barton is originally from Canada but is now based in London, UK, "and in addition to his role in Morneau's Council, is Chair of the Seoul Business Council and the U.S. President's Advisory Council on Doing Business in Africa."[12]

Nerenberg included some pointed remarks about McKinsey & Co., where Dominic Barton is "top man." He wrote: "McKinsey calls itself the global management consulting company – and is it ever global. It has offices in 61 countries: from Saudi Arabia to Kazakhstan, from Nigeria to the Philippines, from Slovakia to Chile to Australia. It operates almost everywhere, including four locations in Canada, and its purpose is to serve its (mostly) corporate clients."[13]

Just what does a "global management consulting company" do?

Nerenberg helpfully explained: "McKinsey provides executive coaching, works to help companies adopt new technologies, helps streamline organizations, and much more. It even advertises itself as a turn-around specialist, taking on failing companies and helping make them profitable again. One of McKinsey's key values is confidentiality. The firm does not publicize the list of its many clients worldwide. Clients can count on the firm's absolute discretion. So we do not know what companies, in what kinds of business, have used McKinsey's service. McKinsey pointedly does not say there are certain businesses that are off limits. It seems to be open to working for any organization with the cash to pay for its services."[14]

Nerenberg added that "you can draw your own conclusions as to the kind of advice [Barton] is likely to give to his friend [Finance Minister] Bill Morneau."

It's important to note that apparently, there are times when a "turn-around specialist" like McKinsey & Co. actually can take a functioning organization and turn it into a disaster. Or at least that seems to be the view across much of England towards McKinsey. Adding heft to this argument is the fact that Dominic Barton told *The Globe and Mail* in 2009, "I believe very much in creative destruction."[15]

Creative Destruction

Over the past few years, people in the UK have been in a pitched battle to save their beloved (publicly-owned) National Health Service (NHS) from the creeping privatization plans outlined largely by McKinsey & Company. As *Management Today* – a publication not known for radicalism – noted in 2013, "McKinsey busies itself below the radar and out of public sight. But in the past year the firm has taken a battering in Britain over its work for the NHS ... There are many within the UK public sector who loathe McKinsey: it is seen as a neo-liberal stooge promoting a market-oriented public sector into which its private clients might be helped to win lucrative contracts."[16]

The anger was fuelled by a 2012 feature in *The Mail on Sunday* entitled "The Firm That Hijacked the NHS," revealing that the controversial *Health and Social Care Bill* was largely based on advice from McKinsey: "Many of the Bill's proposals were drawn up by McKinsey and included in the legislation wholesale. One document says the firm has used its privileged access to 'share information' with its corporate clients – which include the world's biggest private hospital firms – who are now set to bid for health service work."[17]

By that point, McKinsey had already earned at least 13 million pounds from UK government health policy changes (that McKinsey itself seems to have recommended), and the new bill "opens up most of the current 106 billion pounds NHS budget to the private sector, with much of it likely to go to McKinsey clients."[18] A major 2009 report from McKinsey called on the NHS to find "efficiency savings" of 4 billion pounds every year for five years – advice that led to cuts imposed in 2012, including the loss of more than 6,000 nursing jobs.[19]

McKinsey has been pushing the NHS toward the American for-profit healthcare model, and has even taken UK legislators on trips to the U.S. to see the "integrated care model" in action. After one such trip, the chairman of the government's health watchdog (who is now NHS Productivity Minister) emailed to McKinsey that "50 per cent" of UK hospital beds could close. That revelation in autumn 2015 by the *Daily Mirror* sparked a huge outcry. The closure of more than 65,000 hospital beds would be the "single largest cut in the history of the NHS".[20]

UK campaigners attempting to save the NHS from further privatization also warned in autumn 2015 about the controversial U.S.-EU trade deal called TTIP (the Transatlantic Trade and Investment Partnership). Gail Cartmail of Unite told the *Daily Mirror*: "TTIP threatens to make the privatisation of the NHS irreversible by giving US healthcare companies new rights to sue the Government if it ever attempted to take privatised health services back into public ownership. The NHS must be protected from TTIP and private U.S. healthcare companies."[21]

In October 2015, Jeremy Corbyn, Nicola Sturgeon, Nigel Farage, and Natalie Bennett all signed an appeal urging that the NHS be exempted from the TTIP.[22] The Brexit vote to leave the EU came in the midst of this NHS controversy, although most explanations of the referendum results have ignored any connection to saving the NHS.

McKinsey & Company has been largely responsible for the creeping privatization of the NHS, a slow turn-around of an organization that had been functioning well for decades. McKinsey was also involved in other privatizations of state assets in the UK.

So here we must ask: why would the Trudeau Liberals choose Dominic Barton of McKinsey as the "New Economy Czar"? Like the similar question about the Bank of America Merrill Lynch banker advising on a Canada Infrastructure Bank, it doesn't make sense unless there is a larger agenda at work that hasn't been revealed to us serfs.

The "McKinsey Kool-Aid"

One writer for *Jacobin Magazine*, Salem Saif, has referred to the "meteoric rise" of McKinsey over the last decade as it increased privatization worldwide, including in the Gulf states, where it has advised the Kingdom of Bahrain, the United Arab Emirates, Libya, Egypt, Yemen, and (most recently) Saudi Arabia. McKinsey "has made its mark by creating grand plans – 'economic visions' for each country. These master plans present countries with a blueprint to transform their entire economies, promising to move them from oil dependency to rich, 'diversified,' 'knowledge-based' economies."[23]

But Saif noticed a pattern: "many of the countries who drank the McKinsey Kool-Aid became epicenters of the Arab Spring. Bahrain, Egypt, Libya, Yemen – each was convulsed by demonstrations, often animated by economic grievances. Unlike other firms, McKinsey's reputation hasn't suffered from its association with these failed grand plans. It continues to secure lucrative contracts in the region," and elsewhere.[24]

The "McKinsey Kool-Aid" involves "plans to privatize public infrastructure, education and even health care" – which "might be smart strategy from the point of view of corporate shareholders, but it hardly makes sense when reshaping and running a nation's economy. In the neoliberal age, however, where a financial value has to be placed on every object and living being, this does not seem so surprising."[25]

Reportedly, the Saudis sarcastically refer to the world's most prestigious consulting company as the "Ministry of McKinsey" – the company behind the January 2016 announcement by Saudi deputy crown prince Muhammad bin Salman of a plan to privatize oil giant Aramco in order to raise a $2 trillion megafund, starting with a 5% selloff for $100 billion.[26] This is clearly the biggest example of "asset recycling" to date, part of the "Economic Vision 2030" developed by McKinsey for the

Saudi prince.

Have the Trudeau Liberals taken a large sip of the "McKinsey Kool-Aid"? As of September 2016, we don't yet know what's in store from the Economic Advisory Board that Dominic Barton chairs, but it's worth noting that his 14-member team includes Elyse Allan (President and CEO of GE Canada, Vice President of GE, and board member of the C.D. Howe Institute), Brian Ferguson (President and CEO of Cenovus Energy Inc. and board member of TD Bank), and Christopher Ragan (research fellow at the C.D. Howe Institute).

GE's Elyse Allan was a member of the Alberta Premier's Council for Economic Strategy, which in 2011 recommended a deregulated water market for the province. GE is part of the Aqueduct Alliance (with Goldman Sachs and the World Resources Institute), which has been mapping opportunities world-wide for water speculators and investors, and utilizing data provided by Coca-Cola.[27]

GE is also part of the Global Energy Network Institute (GENI), which has long been advocating a massive transformation of the electricity grid in North America and elsewhere, to provide astonishing corporate control of huge regions through grid integration. GE's partners in GENI include the World Bank, Westinghouse (now owned by Toshiba), Pacific Gas & Electric, Mitsubishi, and Siemens. GENI's Peter Meisen told me in 2010 that British Columbia "has much more hydro potential that could be built and exported to the U.S."[28]

So General Electric has quite a vested interest in Canadian infrastructure issues.

In late August 2016, the Economic Advisory Board met again with Morneau to suggest options, including more openness to foreign direct investment in Canada and more involvement with Asia and Africa.[29] The federal Liberals are gearing up for their second budget in February/March 2017, which will lay out details of Phase Two of their big infrastructure plans. Barton is pushing for $500 billion in infrastructure spending – which could be a PR gesture designed to make $120 billion look reasonable.

There may be an additional reason that Barton was selected for this influential post, and it has to do with an important article that the turn-around specialist wrote in 2011.

5. The Turn-Around Specialist

In March 2011, Dominic Barton published an article in the *Harvard Business Review* that received widespread comment and praise from a huge business readership. The article was entitled "Capitalism for the Long Term," and it offered both a dire warning about capitalism's potential demise and a profitable solution to the pending threat.

Since McKinsey & Co. is a turn-around specialist for failing corporations, you could say that the company's top man was offering nothing less than a turn-around strategy to save capitalism itself.

Dominic Barton warned: "The near meltdown of the financial system and the ensuing Great Recession have been, and will remain, the defining issue for the current generation of executives. Now that the worst seems to be behind us, it's tempting to feel deep relief – and a strong desire to return to the comfort of business as usual. But that is simply not an option," he wrote, because "the most consequential outcome of the crisis is the challenge to capitalism itself." [1]

Business executives may have been feeling "relief" by March 2011, and a sense that "the worst" had passed, but those feelings weren't shared by the general population across much of the world. As Barton noted, "the crisis and the surge in public antagonism it unleashed have exacerbated the friction between business and society ... Business leaders today face a choice: We can reform capitalism, or we can let capitalism be reformed for us, through political measures and the pressures of an angry public."[2]

There certainly were reasons for "friction": the massive bank bail-outs; the fact that millions had lost their homes to foreclosures in the U.S.; the fact that millions more (through no fault of their own) had lost their pension funds and retirement savings to Wall Street's gambling casino. As the *Rolling Stone's* Matt Taibbi later reported, "public pension funds were some of the most frequently targeted suckers upon whom Wall Street dumped its fraud-riddled mortgage-backed securities in the pre-crash years."[3] In the U.S. alone, by October 2008 some $2 trillion in retirement savings had been wiped out, and further revelations about lost retirement savings were still to come.[4]

Financial analysts Pam Martens and Russ Martens also reported that "counties and cities and school districts across America" were "similarly fleeced and hoodwinked by investment banks on Wall Street."[5] But it's taken years for such information to come out. In the immediate aftermath of the Wall Street crisis, it's fair to say that confusion reigned supreme.

So yes, in March 2011 Dominic Barton was right: there was definitely an "angry public," and he warned his readers that the Edelman PR agency's "Trust Barometer" for business was at "near-crisis lows" in 2011, especially in the U.S. and the UK.[6] But by 2011, it's also fair to say that a lot of that public anger, at least in the U.S., had been cleverly diverted into the so-called Tea Party movement – a re-direction of public sentiment that may stand as one of the most astonishing PR stunts ever pulled off by Wall Street and the overlords.

"Tea Party" Rise

For many, the origin of the so-called Tea Party movement is lost in the mists of time and spin. Their assumption is that the Tea Party was a truly "populist" movement born out of the righteous anger about the misery that Wall Street banks dumped on everybody but themselves. Many assume that the Tea Party spontaneously evolved out of that anger and grew into a formidable "grassroots" movement that took the U.S. House of Representatives by storm in 2010.

In fact, the Tea Party was as "astroturf" as you can get.

On February 19, 2009, a CNBC business reporter named Rick Santelli was standing on the floor of the Chicago Board of Trade, reporting on aspects of TARP, the Troubled Assets Relief Program being implemented by the newly elected Obama administration. The TARP bank bailout – which handed more than $700 billion in taxpayer dollars to banks – was (and still is) highly controversial. Its structuring had been (at least in part) overseen by BlackRock's Larry Fink.[7]

But on that February day, Santelli had focused on one small aspect of TARP – in fact, the only part of TARP that was actually designed to help homeowners who had been swindled into those sub-prime mortgages. This element of TARP was supposed to modify mortgage terms and prevent foreclosures.

As the CNBC's Santelli reported on this, he managed to work himself into rage at those homeowner "losers" and how TARP would be "promoting bad behavior" and would "subsidize the losers' mortgages" with taxpayer dollars. "This is America!" he yelled. Turning to his friends on the Chicago trading floor, he asked, "How many people want to pay for your neighbor's mortgage that has an extra bathroom and can't pay their bills?" Boo, said the traders, enjoying the rant. Then Santelli invited "all you capitalists" to defy Obama and attend a "Chicago Tea Party" to dump securities into Lake Michigan.

In other words, Santelli was mobilising the traders and financiers against any government bailout of their victims, even while the banks were receiving billions in government money. Santelli's rant went viral, while mainstream media coverage dutifully focused on all the tri-cornered hats and "Don't Tread on Me" protest signs that suddenly blossomed in the wake of Santelli's 15 minutes of fame.

As Thomas Frank later observed in his book *Pity the Billionaire*, "In different times, the TARP might have become the rallying point of a revitalized Left," because the TARP gave the banks whatever they wanted. "Had they mobilized themselves quickly, [left] reformers might have depicted the TARP as the final chapter in the great book of fraud," where bankers transferred their debts to the public. "But it was the Right that grabbed the opportunity to define the debate," shifting the burden of villainy "from Wall Street to government."[8]

The Guardian's George Monbiot later noted that "on the same day" as Rick Santelli's CNBC rant, "a group called Americans for Prosperity (AFP) set up a Tea Party Facebook page and started organising Tea Party events ... [AFP] was founded and is funded by Charles and David Koch," the right-wing billionaire brothers now known for their Kochtopus of front groups. "AFP mobilised the anger of people who found their conditions of life declining, and channelled it into a campaign to make them worse. Tea Party campaigners take to the streets to demand less tax for billionaires and worse health care, education and social insurance for themselves. Are they stupid? No. They have been misled by another instrument of corporate power: the media," especially Fox News, owned by billionaire Rupert Murdoch.[9]

But in 2009, confusion reigned and none of this was widely known at all. Even by early 2011, when McKinsey's Dominic Barton was writing his article warning about the crisis of capitalism, it's fair to say that, in North America at least, the Left hadn't organized any kind of resistance except to work to get political candidates re-elected. Occupy Wall Street was still months in the future.

So it seems important to ask: as of March 2011, what was prompting Dominic Barton to warn that "if we merely paper over the cracks [of capitalism] and return to our pre-crisis views, we will not want to read what the historians of the future will write"?[10] I suspect that what may have motivated Barton was a series of major events in 2010, including a literary phenomenon across the pond by which a frail if dapper nonagenarian was proving to be a significant threat.

6. Year of Our Overlords 2010

The Tea Party movement was rolling across the U.S., raising ire against The Government, not the banksters, and calling for serfs to demand protection for free markets, respect for private property rights, the dismantling of regulations, prevention of a "debt ceiling crisis" – causes that the oligarchy itself supported.

An enormous Labor Day rally had been held in West Virginia in 2009 to show just how committed U.S. corporations are to workers, especially with regard to "government meddling." Tea Party favorites Sean Hannity and Ted Nugent attended the rally, which was paid for and presided over by Don Blankenship, the CEO of Massey Energy. Blankenship appeared on stage dressed in (of course) American flag clothing and told the crowd that he was there to "defend American labor" and to stand tall against governments whose safety and environmental regulations are "American workers' worst nightmare."[1]

Just eight months after that rally, however, on April 5, 2010 a huge underground explosion at Massey Energy's Upper Big Branch (UBB) mine in West Virginia took the lives of 29 miners – one of the worst disasters in U.S. mining history. In the months before the fiery explosion, the UBB mine had logged "50 safety violations, many related to ventilation." Survivors reported that "workers who tried to get dangerous conditions addressed were ignored, threatened or told to tamper with monitoring equipment. A union safety committee could have stopped work at UBB. But there was no union at UBB."[2] Blankenship "had made it his personal business to keep out the United Mine Workers of America," despite the fact that "70 per cent of the workers had signed union cards."[3]

As the dust was settling on that tragedy, another disaster shook the public's confidence in the corporate sector. On April 21, 2010, BP's Deepwater Horizon offshore drilling rig exploded in the Gulf of Mexico, killing 11 workers and spewing four billion gallons of oil into the Gulf. For nearly three months, TV viewers around the world watched horrifying images of the oil pouring into the ocean. Then in July, another disaster happened, in Michigan: Canadian firm Enbridge's tar sands pipeline leaked millions of gallons of toxic diluted bitumen (dilbit) into the Kalamazoo River – the worst on-land oil disaster in U.S. history.

No doubt, global management consultant Dominic Barton was taking note of these events from his lofty perch at McKinsey & Co.

While BP's oil disaster was underway, a strange event occurred that shook the financial world and may also have caught Barton's attention.

"Flash Crash"

On the afternoon of May 6, 2010, the stock market suddenly fell six hundred points for no apparent reason. A few minutes later, it just as suddenly soared right back up to where it had been – again, for no reason. But during those intervening minutes, thousands of stock trades had occurred at prices markedly different from those quoted just moments beforehand.

It was the stock market's first "flash crash," an event that may have gone unnoticed by the vast public (which can barely pay the bills, much less play the stock market). But for others, this "flash crash" eventually revealed just how insidious "high-frequency trading" (HFT) had become, with some traders technologically poised to game the system by "front-running" (getting in front of the orders of ordinary investors) through their high-speed nanosecond advantage. As author Michael

Lewis later wrote, "The U.S. stock market was now a class system, rooted in speed, of haves and have-nots. The haves paid for nanoseconds; the have-nots had no idea that a nanosecond had value."[4]

Lewis' *Flash Boys* would go a long way toward explaining just what HFT means, but it wouldn't be published until 2013, long after that first "flash crash." In the meantime, however, Lewis' book, *The Big Short,* had quickly risen to the bestseller list in 2010 and it greatly added to the public's understanding of the crash. You could even say that Lewis helped to reframe Wall Street's own reframing of what had happened in 2008 as the banks (and the Tea Party) began to claim that they had been forced to take bailouts by the big, bad intrusive government.

In 2010 Lewis wrote, "The events on Wall Street in 2008 were soon reframed, not just by Wall Street leaders but also by both the U.S. Treasury and the Federal Reserve, as a 'crisis in confidence'," a simple financial panic caused by the fall of Lehman Brothers. But Lewis noted that every Wall Street firm was bankrupt or part of the bankrupt system, so the "problem wasn't that Lehman Brothers had been allowed to fail. The problem was that Lehman Brothers had been allowed to succeed."[5]

As Matt Taibbi later wrote about the run-up to the 2008 crash, "This was a massive criminal fraud scheme, something akin to a giant counterfeiting operation, in which banks mass-produced extremely risky, low-quality subprime mortgages and with lightning-quick efficiency sold them off to institutional sucker-investors as high rated AAA bonds. The hot-potato game targeted unions, pension funds and government-backed mortgage companies like Fannie Mae on the secondary market."[6]

Those "sucker-investors" were quickly wising up by 2010 and likely buying copies of Michael Lewis' *The Big Short*, where he wrote, "This new [bailout] regime – free money for capitalists, free markets for everyone else – plus the more or less instant rewriting of financial history vexed all sorts of people."[7]

I imagine that, as he read his copy of *The Big Short* in 2010, McKinsey CEO Dominic Barton must have been racking his brain for the big turn-around that obviously was going to be needed – because those "sucker-investors" were not just American unions, pension funds, and communities; they were all over the world.

Globalizing "Sucker-Investors"

Pension and other investors across the planet had been sucked into the toxic assets vortex by a little-known change in something called the *Financial Services Agreement* (FSA) – a part of the World Trade Organisation (WTO) agreements governing international trade.

Back in 1997-9 during the Bill Clinton administration, U.S. Treasury Secretary Robert Rubin pushed to deregulate U.S. banks by repealing the *Glass-Steagall Act*, which dismantled the barrier between commercial banks and investment banks. This move allowed the banks to engage in the new high-risk game of "derivatives trading," which then-Deputy Treasury Secretary Larry Summers protected from any attempts at regulatory controls.

But the U.S. financial sector wanted to play a much larger game. So Larry Summers and a handful of bankers in 1997-1999 lobbied for a rewrite of the rules of the WTO's *Financial Services Agreement*, making changes that thereby forced all 156 nations that were WTO signatories to dismantle their own versions of *Glass-Steagall*.

As Greg Palast later explained, "Until the bankers began their play, the WTO agreements dealt simply with trade in goods – that is, my cars for your bananas. The new rules devised by Summers and the banks would force all nations to accept trade in 'bads' – toxic assets like financial derivatives. Until the bankers' re-draft of the FSA, each nation controlled and chartered the banks within their own borders. The new rules of the game would force every nation to open their markets to Citibank, JP Morgan and their derivatives 'products' ... The job of turning the FSA into the bankers' [global] battering ram was given to [Timothy] Geithner, who was [later] named Ambassador to the World Trade Organisation."[8] Geithner had been the Assistant Secretary to Larry Summers at the Treasury Department.

Without that rewrite of the WTO's *Financial Services Agreement*, Wall Street's toxic assets could not have been flogged across the world.

The intrepid Greg Palast obtained a confidential 1997 Treasury Department Memo that, as he put it, "confirmed every conspiracy freak's fantasy: that in the late 1990s, the US Treasury officials secretly conspired with a small cabal of banker big-shots to rip apart financial regulation across the planet."[9] The November 24, 1997 Memo was from Timothy Geithner (then Assistant Secretary at Treasury) to his boss Larry Summers (then Deputy Secretary), reminding him that they were entering "the end-game of WTO financial services negotiations" and that Summers should "touch base with the CEOs."[10]

As Palast wrote, "Larry Summer's flunky, Timothy Geithner [was] reminding his boss to call the Bank big shots to order their lobbyist armies to march ... To avoid Summers having to call his office to get the phone numbers (which, under U.S. law, would have to appear on public logs), Geithner listed the private lines of what were then the five most powerful CEOs on the planet."[11] The five were Goldman Sachs' John Corzine, Merrill Lynch's David Kamanski, Bank of America's David Coulter, Citibank's John Reed, and Chase Manhattan's Walter Shipley.[12]

According to Palast, "It's not the little cabal of confabs held by Summers and the banksters [in 1997] that's so troubling. The horror is in the purpose of the 'end game' itself" – all those WTO signatory nations were "bullied into signing" the changes and forced to open their banking systems to U.S. derivatives trading.[13] Of those 156 WTO nations, only one, Brazil, did not sign the changes to the *Financial Services Agreement*.

After the FSA rewrite, Wall Street's "new financial products were packaged, polished to a shine, and sold to government pension funds all over the planet. The bankers sold blind sacks of sub-prime mortgages, sliced and mixed up, as Collateralized Debt Obligations (CDOs) and other fetid concoctions. The *Financial Services Agreement* was rockin'! But when opened, buyers found the bags were filled with financial feces. Government pensions and sovereign [wealth] funds, from Finland to Qatar, lost trillions. The bags were toxic to bank balance sheets and several [foreign] banks failed. However, in most cases, bankers could get a refill of capital juice from governments fearful of full-bore financial collapse. Re-funding banks meant de-funding economies: pension cuts, salary cuts, all the things that bring an economy to its knees."[14]

In Canada we now know that from 2008 to 2010 at least $108 billion had been quietly provided by the Harper government to bailout Canada's biggest banks.

Some of those WTO signatory nations in Europe who approved the late 1990s FSA changes had earlier signed the Maastricht Treaty, agreeing to keep their budget deficits to 3% of national income and their debt levels at 60% of GDP. For them, the 2008 Wall Street meltdown was even more disastrous. "When the bottom fell out during the 2008 economic meltdown, EU states found out just what they had signed on for: draconian austerity measures, the widespread privatization of state owned enterprises – from water and electrical systems, to airports and harbors – and emigration. Millions of mainly young Portuguese, Irish, Greeks and Spaniards fled abroad."[15]

Former Treasury Secretary Robert Rubin went on to campaign and raise funds for a young senator named Barack Obama, who, after his 2008 election as President, named Larry Summers as his "Economics Czar" and appointed Tim Geithner as his Secretary of Treasury, along with a host of others connected to Robert Rubin. As Matt Taibbi wrote, "Taken together, the rash of appointments with ties to Bob Rubin may well represent the most sweeping influence by a single Wall Street insider in the history of government."[16] For those paying attention, these were ominous signals.

"This Ain't Canada"

You could say that by the Year of Our Overlords 2010, amidst all the chaos there was also a new interest in financial and economic matters, as people scrambled to understand not just "collateral debt obligations" (which nobody in their right mind could understand) but also the larger realm of finance capital and its globalized workings.

In Canada, the G-20 Summit held in Toronto (June 26-27, 2010) cast further negative light on governments' handling of economic and monetary issues. As world leaders gathered to discuss the economy, the Stephen Harper government mounted the largest and most expensive security operation in Canadian history: spending $1.8 billion on security costs for policing the 10,000 mostly peaceful protesters who turned out to advocate for a global banking tax, a Robin Hood tax on high-speed financial transactions, and other measures to reign in global capital.

The police responded by arresting more than 1,100 citizens – the largest mass arrests in Canadian history – with widespread police brutality and violations of civil rights.

In one infamous example posted to YouTube, Police Sgt. Mark Charlebois told peaceful protestors, "This ain't Canada right now ... There is no civil rights here in this area," as he arrested them for being too close to the security fence.

On the streets, the police tried out a new tactic called "kettling": totally surrounding hundreds of protestors and pedestrians at a major intersection and blocking them from leaving for hours, even during a torrential downpour. Finally, the police opened one path from the "kettle," herding many directly into waiting paddy-wagons.

Not only were the people of Toronto shocked by the police response, but most Canadians were outraged that the Harper government had treated its citizens with such disdain, spending multiple times more on security than any other G-20 host government had ever done.

Meanwhile, inside the G-20 Summit, both Canada and the U.S. opposed any new tax on the global banking sector and managed to convince other nations to increase their austerity measures. While protesters were being strip-searched and caged in detention centres, or pepper-sprayed, tear-gassed, and kettled on downtown Toronto streets, the leaders of the developed world were agreeing to protect the financial oligarchs and punish the rest with further austerity cuts.

Time for Outrage

While Lewis' *The Big Short* shot to the top of bestseller lists in the U.S. in 2010, another literary creation in Europe was fast becoming a publishing phenomenon – one even more challenging for corporate capitalism itself.

The work was entitled *Indignez-Vous!* and it was a mere 40 pages long. The pamphlet had quickly sold more than 600,000 copies in a few weeks, and at least 4.5 million copies in 35 countries within a few months. Even more amazing, the writer was not some young blogger taking on the establishment and sparking web-based "clicktivism." The author was a somewhat frail but dapper 93-year-old man named Stephane Hessel, and the work was published in the same time-worn way as most political treatises over the last few centuries: by the printing press.

Hessel's 2010 pamphlet was translated into English as *Time for Out-*

rage. The work was originally written as a speech to commemorate the resistance to Hitler's occupation of France during World War II. Hessel had been a prominent member of the French Resistance, and the aim of his speech (and the 2010 pamphlet) was to inspire contemporary youth with the same passion with which his generation had resisted the Nazis.

No doubt, Hessel had what they call "street cred," not just with youth but with everyone. As a Resistance fighter during World War II, he had been arrested and tortured by the Gestapo and deported to Buchenwald and then Dora concentration camps, before escaping en route to the Bergen-Belsen death camp.[17]

Hessel's pamphlet touches on numerous issues including environmental degradation, rising inequality, loss of civil rights, ill-treatment of immigrants, and Israeli attacks on Palestinians. But Hessel also urged people to "not give up or be overwhelmed by the current international dictatorship of the financial markets, which is such a threat to peace and democracy."[18] And here's where Hessel's pamphlet was so important: he reminded his French readers of a time in their recent history when public banking had transformed their society.

Hessel recalled for his readers that the National Council of the Resistance had successfully insisted on "a comprehensive Social Security plan," and a sweeping programme that included nationalizing the French banks.[19] Hessel summarized that programme: "Sources of energy – electricity, gas, coal – were nationalised, along with the large banks," in order to remove "large-scale economic and 'financial feudalism from the management of the economy'."[20]

In fact, in 1946 the French federal treasury began borrowing interest-free from the nationalized Banque de France – just like Canadian governments were borrowing interest-free from the Bank of Canada – and the French government did this until 1973, when the "law was changed to forbid this practice, requiring the treasury to borrow instead from the private sector."[21]

Hessel thereby revealed part of the hidden history of France: that it was actually the Resistance that had achieved "an ambitious resurrection" of the country, and that it had done so by mandating interest-free loans for government spending.[22] He told his readers: "The power of money which the resistance fought so hard against has never been as great and selfish and shameless as it is now," and he urged young people to "take over, keep going, get angry."[23]

The timing of Hessel's 2010 work was fortuitous, coming out at a time of growing resistance against imposed austerity programs across Europe. In Spain, protesters took on the name Los Indignados, inspired by the title of Hessel's pamphlet.

The "Social Contract"

With offices in 61 countries, McKinsey & Company's Dominic Barton was likely well aware of the *Time for Outrage* publishing phenomenon as it spread across the world in its dozens of translations. One of the jobs of a global management consultant is to know what's happening that could affect their corporate clients, especially if they're failing.

In his piece for March 2011 *Harvard Business Review*, Barton doesn't mention Hessel and *Time for Outrage* (or Michael Lewis' *The Big Short*, for that matter), but he does state that, "In an ongoing effort that started 18 months ago, I've met with more than 400 business and government leaders across the globe" and found a "growing concern that if the fundamental issues revealed in the crisis remain unaddressed and the system fails again, the social contract between the capitalist system and the citizenry may truly rupture, with unpredictable but severely damaging results."[24]

Any number of serfs could have told Barton that the so-called "social contract" had ruptured some time ago, although there might have been squabbling about just when and where that first happened. With rising homelessness across much of the UK and Europe; with former middle-class professionals in Spain, Italy and Greece foraging through dumpsters for food; with youth unemployment escalating across North America and Europe; with wages across North America stuck at 1970s levels; with farmers in Mexico going bankrupt because of cheap corn imports dumped on their markets; with ten million Americans foreclosed on their homes and other millions losing their pension funds, it was hard to see just where that so-called "social contract" had not already been "ruptured," except in corporate boardrooms with their escalating bonuses and salaries.

Indeed, Barton had only to look at Edelman's most recent "Trust Barometer" (which he cites) to see that "trust in business in the U.S. and the UK (although up from mid-crisis record lows) is only in the vicinity of 45%." So, he wrote, "How can business leaders restore the public's trust? Many Western executives find that nothing in their careers has prepared them for this new challenge."[25]

"Quarterly Capitalism"

In order to "reform" capitalism, Barton called for "nothing less than a shift from what I call quarterly capitalism to what might be referred to as long-term capitalism." He explained that "quarterly capitalism" – with its focus on quarterly reports, quarterly earnings targets, overnight stock-market results, short-term performance ratings, and high-speed trading – was part of the "short-termism" that had overtaken business, to its own peril.[26]

He wrote, "To break free of the tyranny of short-termism, we must start with those who provide capital. Taken together, pension funds, insurance companies, mutual funds, and sovereign wealth funds hold $65 trillion, or roughly 35% of the world's financial assets. If these players focus too much attention on the short term, capitalism as a whole will, too." By contrast Barton mentioned that Mark Wiseman at the Canada Pension Plan Investment Board "advocated investing 'for the next quarter century,' not the next quarter. And Warren Buffett has quipped that his ideal holding period is 'forever.' Still, these remain admirable exceptions."[27]

Barton was especially insistent about the need for companies to engage with groups outside the financial industry and foster "social initiatives" that appeal to the social sector. The passage seems a bit quaint – dare I say out of touch? – as though unions and NGOs hadn't been dealing with corporate spin-doctors and their "social initiatives" for decades. But Barton was clearly addressing a large cross-section of business colleagues, some of whom in 2011 may have had no experience with spin-doctoring.

Well, apparently the piece was seen as a remarkable 2011 clarion call for business leaders (and especially investors) to change not only their own outlook but their corporate culture.

Barton offered a number of examples of "Who's Getting It Right?" in terms of thinking long-term as of 2011, mentioning initiatives by Verizon, Wal-Mart, General Electric, and Coca-Cola, and he quoted Black-Rock's Larry Fink who, during a 2009 *Financial Times* debate about the future of capitalism, had stated, "I actually don't think risk management failed ... I think corporate governance failed, because ... the boards didn't ask the right questions."[28]

Dominic Barton's piece was widely read and likely got business leaders thinking in a new way about how to lock in profits for the long-term, while keeping shareholders happy and stakeholders in check. Succinctly summarizing, Barton wrote: "Getting capital more aligned with capitalism should help businesses enrich shareholders by better serving stakeholders."[29]

It was one of those quotable quotes that business editors and pundits look for, with a nice rhythm and sentiment to it. But some may have wondered: If capital hasn't been aligned with capitalism, just what has it been aligned with?

7. Zuccotti Park and the Meme Warriors

The first years of the Great Recession can be characterized as essentially a Great Race, with the banks and their supporters working mightily to spin the events on Wall Street in their own way, and others working just as feverishly to understand and explain just what the hell had happened, and why.

The latter group – including business reporters, analysts and commentators – was at a severe disadvantage, having little access to the in-house records or meetings of the Wall Street titans, or the dialing-for-dollars deals underway in the White House. But for every Rick Santelli venting on CNBC against foreclosed "losers," there was some journalist or reporter (like Matt Taibbi at *Rolling Stone*) doggedly trying to dig through the mess and explain.

You could say that this Great Race was a classic example of what Naomi Klein's bestseller *The Shock Doctrine* had delineated: how "disaster capitalism" works during chaos to seize the advantage.[1]

With Stephane Hessel's *Indignez-vous!* urging youth to resist "the international dictatorship of finance capitalism," throughout 2011 there were passionate protests across France, England, Iceland, Ireland, Greece, and Spain. Then in late September 2011, an independent market trader named Alessio Rastani appeared on the BBC and bluntly told the host of the show, "The governments don't rule the world, Goldman Sachs rules the world."[2] The gobsmacked BBC host told him, "If you could see the people around me, jaws have collectively dropped at what you just said." Rastani continued, "For most traders we don't really care that much how they are going to fix the economy. Our job is to make money from it."

New Meme

So there it was, out in the open: Goldman Sachs rules the world. As the financial industry scrambled to smear the remark as a hoax – and the market trader as a possible a member of the satirical group Yes Men – the meme was travelling around the planet, thanks to social media. In a way, "Goldman Sachs rules the world" was becoming another "flash crash," but this one (momentarily or otherwise) bringing down not the stock market but conventional thinking: "The governments don't rule the world, Goldman Sachs rules the world."

No doubt, that meme was being excitedly exchanged among Occupy Wall Street (OWS) activists, who had taken over Manhattan's Zuccotti Park (owned by Canadian firm Brookfield Properties, part of Brookfield Asset Management) on September 17, 2011 and were promoting their own meme: "We are the 99%."

Indeed, as I read OWS's first official statement (October 10, 2011), I can't help but think of Rastani's remark on the BBC. Near the beginning of the OWS statement we find this: "We come to you at a time when corporations, which place profit over people, self-interest over justice, and oppression over equality, run our governments. We have peaceably assembled here, as is our right, to let these facts be known."[3] There then follows a long list of corporate malfeasance, ranging from the banker bailouts to animal cruelty to creating weapons of mass destruction.

This isn't the place (and I'm not the one) to offer a critique of the Occupy Movement, which was launched by Kalle Lasn and Micah White of *Adbusters* magazine, based in Vancouver, B.C. That critique has already been attempted by at least three books.[4] For the record, I think the Occupy Movement has made (and continues to make) great contributions to society, including a meme that still hasn't gone down the memory-hole. Getting anything about class issues into the mainstream is a major accomplishment, and for that alone OWS deserves our thanks.

Rather than criticize OWS, I think it's important to examine the financial sector's response to OWS, which was after all a challenge to the oligarchy. To do that, it's necessary to keep in mind that Dominic Barton's article about the need to reform capitalism in order to save it had been avidly discussed for six months before OWS set up in Zuccotti Park.

Moreover, the overlords likely knew something big was coming. Aside from the Stephane Hessel-inspired protests across Europe, on February 2, 2011, the *Adbusters* website posted a call for an upcoming "Million Man March on Wall Street." The overlords had months to prepare for it.

Unlikely Allies

In 2013, long after OWS sites had been emptied (usually by force), the *Financial Times* claimed that unlike the "anarchist core" of the OWS Movement, "most of its supporters did not turn up because they rejected the bourgeois promises inherent in the American dream or European social democracy. Rather, they came because they were cheated of those promises."[5]

Stephane Hessel remarked in an interview given in 2012 (a year before he died), "The global protest movement does not resemble the Communist movement, which declared that the world had to be overturned according to its viewpoint." Instead, he said, "This is not an ideological revolution. It is driven by an authentic desire to get what you need. From this point of view, the present generation is not asking governments to disappear but change the way they deal with people's needs."[6]

As the *Toronto Star's* Linda McQuaig observed, "part of the Occupiers' point is that democracy has become a hollow shell ... In particular, as the Occupiers note, the concentration of wealth in the hands of the top 1 per cent undermines meaningful democracy, blocking the will of the bottom 99 per cent," at the same time that "the fundamental dysfunction of our economic system" also "massively favours a privileged elite at the expense of the rest."[7]

In the early days of OWS, along with mass arrests and police brutality, there were expressions of sympathy from the unlikeliest of allies: millionaires and billionaires. Bill Gross, who runs a $1.2 trillion bond fund called Pacific Investment Management Co. (Pimco), called OWS an "unsurprising reaction" to the class war, while BlackRock's Larry Fink said of OWS: "These are not lazy people sitting around looking for something to do. We have people losing hope and they're going into the street, whether it's justified or not."[8]

Former Canadian prime minister Paul Martin also expressed his support of OWS, telling Linda McQuaig that he "sees 'considerable value' in the Occupy movement. 'Everybody I've talked to feels the same way. The question of inequality and the top 1 per cent. That's not what built North America. The fact is [the Occupiers] have touched a chord with Canadians and, I'm sure, with Americans,' said Martin. 'Look, there's something fundamentally wrong here .... For the last hundred years, certainly in North America, every generation has felt it's going to have a better life than their parents. For the first time, that's not there'."

McQuaig reminded her readers that Paul Martin, as finance minister in the 1990s, had "slashed social spending in the name of deficit reduction" – a move completely in line with Milton Friedman's neoliberal economic model – and she noted that Paul Martin "is also very much part of the top 1 per cent."[9]

Rolling Stone's Matt Taibbi concisely shot down the prevailing "propaganda" that OWS protesters were motivated by "envy of the rich." In an Oct. 25, 2011 piece that now seems prescient, Taibbi wrote: "Americans for the most part love the rich, even the obnoxious rich. And in recent years, the harder things got, the more we've obsessed over the wealth dream. As unemployment skyrocketed, people tuned in in droves to gawk at Ovremonde-heiresses like Paris Hilton, or watch bullies like Donald Trump fire people on TV. Moreover, the worse the economy got, the more being a millionaire or a billionaire somehow became a qualification for high office, as people flocked to voting booths to support politicians with names like Bloomberg and Rockefeller and Corzine, names that to voters symbolized success and expertise at a time when few people seemed to have answers. At last count, there were 245 millionaires in congress, including 66 in the Senate. And we hate the rich?

Come on. Success is the national religion, and almost everyone is a be-liever. Americans love winners. But that's just the problem. These guys on Wall Street are not winning – they're cheating. And as much as we love the self-made success story, we hate the cheater that much more."[10]

Taibbi then gave a lengthy summary of Wall Street cheating, includ-ing the fact that "Bank of America last year [2010] paid not a single dollar in taxes – in fact, it received a 'tax credit' of $1 billion," and he ended by saying of OWS, "It's not a class uprising and they don't want civil war – they want just the opposite. They want everyone to live in the same country, and live by the same rules. It's amazing that some people think that that's asking a lot."[11]

The very next day the *New York Times'* Nicholas Kristof offered his own defense of OWS, arguing that it "highlights the need to restore basic capitalist principles like accountability" and it provides "a chance to save capitalism from crony capitalists."[12] He wrote: "It's not just rabble-rous-ers at Occupy Wall Street who are seeking to put America's capitalists on a more capitalist footing," and he cited a recent speech by former Federal Reserve chair Paul Volcker as well as a comment by the Pacific Investment Management Co. (Pimco) CEO, who had told Kristof "that the economic system needs to move toward 'inclusive capitalism' and embrace broad-based job creation while curbing excessive inequality."[13]

Instead of Wall Street "cheaters" and "crony capitalists," there was a desperate need for "inclusive capitalism," or so the emerging narra-tive-framing would have it.

"Crony Capitalism"

In mid-October 2011, financial critic Pam Martens revealed an as-tonishing fact on her blog: Wall Street bankers were spying on OWS protesters through live-video feeds into a tax-funded surveillance centre. Martens wrote: "Wall Street's audacity to corrupt knows no bounds and the cooptation of government by the 1 per cent knows no limits. How else to explain $150 million of taxpayer money going to equip a govern-ment facility in lower Manhattan where Wall Street firms, serially charged with corruption, get to sit alongside the New York Police Department and spy on law abiding citizens."[14]

The surveillance center, called the Lower Manhattan Security Coordination Center, operates round-the-clock and is jointly staffed and operated by the New York Police Department (NYPD) and representatives from Goldman Sachs, Citigroup, JPMorgan Chase, the Federal Reserve, the New York Stock Exchange, and other major Wall Street firms, who each have their own cubicles in the facility with their corporate names on plaques.

According to Martens, "2,000 private spy cameras owned by Wall Street firms, together with approximately 1,000 more owned by the NYPD, are relaying live video feeds of people on the streets in lower Manhattan" to the Center, where they are analyzed. "The project has been funded by New York City taxpayers as well as all U.S. taxpayers through grants from the Federal Department of Homeland Security." In a chilling note, Martens added: "One puzzle has at least been solved. Wall Street's criminals have not been indicted or sent to jail because they have effectively become the police."[15]

It was a remarkable revelation of "crony capitalism" of the worst sort, but the mainstream press did not pick up on it (if they even saw Marten's blog), perhaps because that Lower Manhattan Security Coordination Center had already become "old news."

In a later posting, Martens wrote: "On September 25, 2011, just eight days after the Occupy Wall Street protests began in Zuccotti Park in lower Manhattan, the much acclaimed CBS New Program, 60 Minutes, aired a fawning look at the thousands of surveillance cameras affixed to the buildings and lampposts through New York City" and relaying live images to the surveillance center. The thrust of the 60 Minutes program was "the fine job of counter terrorism being done by the NYPD and its Commissioner, Raymond Kelly. It was a triumph in public relations for a police department about to go on an assault spree – pepper spraying and punching peaceful protestors; kicking, ramming and arresting journalists attempting to cover the Occupy Wall Street demonstrations."[16]

What the 60 Minutes program didn't tell viewers, Martens wrote, was that the surveillance center "is jointly staffed and operated by the NYPD along with the largest Wall Street firms – the same firms under investigation in 50 states for mortgage and foreclosure fraud and widely credited with causing the Nation's economic collapse." The Wall Street firms "bailed out by the 99% are now policing the 99%," Martens stressed.[17]

It's hard to think of a more threatening example of Corporatism, or government colluding with finance capital, than this. But Martens' blog postings garnered little attention at the time. Meanwhile, the billionaire twosome of Larry Fink and Bill Gross were out defending OWS and apparently serving as avatars of "inclusive capitalism."

"Fringe Element Symmetry"

BlackRock's Larry Fink and Pacific Investment Management Co. (Pimco) CEO Bill Gross appeared on Bloomberg News on November 21, 2011, just days after Zuccotti Park had been closed to overnight camping (which thereby dispersed Manhattan protesters to occupy other sites).

Fink spoke first. "I'm actually very happy with Occupy Wall Street because I think that actually for the first time in three years we may have fringe element symmetry. The Tea Party, in my view, said a lot of really good things, but it did shape the 2010 elections in a really big way and I was personally surprised that we didn't have a left-wing element ... I'm not saying I agree with one side or the other; I agree with a lot of fringe elements and what they're trying to say ... and they're basically saying: 'We are unhappy with where we are today, we need to have change and many people have been left behind'."[18]

Fink continued: "We have to admit, as members of the financial press and the financial community, we really did let down a lot of people. There was a huge amount of confidence that Washington was going to protect us and the engine of that protection was through the financial community. And frankly, we let people down ... To resolve this we have to admit it."[19]

Bill Gross then said, "For a long time, for 20 or 30 years, capital has benefitted at the expense of labor ... To not have sympathy with Main Street as opposed to Wall Street is to have blinders."[20] He then went on to criticize "K Street" - the Washington location of many corporate lobbyists and major PR firms. "The fact is that Washington is dominated by K Street, and it's dominated by finance and contributions from large corporations which don't have the interests of Main Street," he said. "We can disagree in terms of solutions," whether "private sector as opposed to public sector," but there was no question about the need of "sympathy for labor as opposed to capital."[21]

Well, it sure seemed as though BlackRock's Larry Fink and Pimco's Bill Gross were speaking truth to power (as they say) – not just defending OWS but speaking on behalf of all those millions of Main Street folks who had lost their jobs, their pensions, their homes to Wall Street greed. If viewers weren't quite sure just what to make of Fink's remark about "fringe element symmetry" (which got a laugh from the live studio audience), nonetheless it was gratifying to have two such successful (very rich!) men voicing sympathy for the people that "Washington and the financial community" had "let down."

Granted, they hadn't said anything about a redistribution of wealth, taxes on banksters, or any other changes, but at least they had recognized that people are "unhappy" and that "capital had benefitted from labor" for decades, however vague that sounded.

But viewers may also have been wondering: If OWS wasn't very scary at all, then why such a violent crackdown on them?

Real "Crony Capitalism"

It can take years for important facts to emerge which expose the actual situation underlying an important event. In military conflict, they call it "the fog of war," as honest journalists struggle to get the facts. In the case of OWS, it wouldn't be until the end of 2012 that important documents emerged that shed light on just how far Corporatism's reach had extended.

In late December 2012, writer Naomi Wolf published a piece in UK's *The Guardian*, revealing "totally integrated corporate-state repression" of OWS. She wrote: "It was more sophisticated than we had imagined: new documents show that the violent crackdown on Occupy last fall – so mystifying at the time – was not just coordinated at the level of the FBI, the Department of Homeland Security [DHS], and local police. The crackdown, which involved, as you may recall, violent arrests, group disruption, canister missiles to the skulls of protesters, people held in handcuffs so tight they were injured, people held in bondage till they were forced to wet or soil themselves – was coordinated with the big banks themselves."[22]

The heavily redacted documents, obtained by a non-profit NGO called Partnership for Civil Justice Fund (PCJF) through an FOI request, showed "a terrifying network of coordinated DHS, FBI, police, regional fusion center, and private-sector activity so completely merged into one another that the monstrous whole is, in fact, one entity: in some cases, bearing a single name, the Domestic Security Alliance Council."[23]

The Domestic Security Alliance Council members at the time included executives of 29 major corporations, including Bank of America, Barclay's, General Electric, and Wal-Mart.[24] Those last two firms had been touted by Dominic Barton as "doing it right for the long-term," which takes on unintended irony in retrospect.

Wolf noted, "The documents, in short, show the cops and DHS working for and with banks to target, arrest, and politically disable peaceful American citizens."[25] PCJF executive director Mara Verheyden-Hilliard told Wolf that the documents showed that the FBI considered OWS a "terrorist threat" and were "conducting surveillance against the movement even as early as August 2011, a month prior to the establishment of the OWS encampment in Zuccotti Park." Verheyden-Hilliard pointed out "the close partnering of banks, the New York Stock Exchange and at least one local Federal Reserve with the FBI and DHS," and she stated that the "documents also show these federal agencies functioning as a de facto intelligence arm of Wall Street and Corporate America."[26]

As *The Guardian's* subhead summarized, "New documents prove what was once dismissed as paranoid fantasy: totally integrated corporate-state repression of dissent." So, protesting OWS youth calling for elected governments to work on behalf of the 99% instead of the 1% was "terrorism."

Of course, some would have said that by not donning tri-cornered hats, those people were suspicious right from the start.

The New Meme

The new meme, "inclusive capitalism," seemed to have legs (as they say), and in 2012 it became the subject of an op-ed in *The Guardian* written by Dominic Barton and Lynn Forester de Rothschild (billionaire CEO of investment firm E. L. Rothschild LLC and friend of the Clintons).[27] Lady de Rothschild then joined the advisory board of Focusing Capital on the Long Term (the think tank formed in 2013 by McKinsey & Co. and the Canada Pension Plan Investment Board).

By May 2014, it was time for the big event: the Conference on Inclusive Capitalism, convened by Lady de Rothschild in the City of London and featuring such luminaries as Prince Charles, Bill Clinton, Bank of England governor Mark Carney, the IMF's Christine Lagarde, and Larry Summers, all speaking about "caring capitalism" to 250 business delegates "representing assets under management of about $30 trillion."[28]

The one-day event must have been glorious, but only weeks later, it became a messy fight about "surplus funds" and unpaid bills and "failure to account for the monies received," with Lady de Rothschild suing the organization that helped her run the conference.[29]

Apparently, the "short-termism" mindset had risen again, sabotaging the best-laid plans.

8. COMER & the National Memory

While that aging nonagenarian in France, Stephane Hessel, was shaking up Europe with his best-selling treatise *Time For Outrage*, another wise old man, in Toronto, was about to launch his own revolutionary action in the form of a lawsuit. Defying all stereotypes about elders, William Krehm was 97 years of age in 2011 when he, as co-founder of COMER, the think tank's Chair Ann Emmett, and COMER took legal action to force the Bank of Canada (BOC) to return to its original mandate of providing near interest-free loans to the federal, provincial, and (potentially) municipal governments.

COMER's Ann Emmett told me during a phone interview that it was Krehm who contacted constitutional lawyer Rocco Galati and convinced him to take on the legal case. Galati is considered one of the top constitutional lawyers in Canada, and he is admired by many for his long-standing fight for justice on numerous issues. In May 2015, Galati and his colleague Joseph Groia were both elected as Law Society of Upper Canada benchers, meaning that they now help set policy for the regulatory body and can sit on disciplinary panels.

Galati told the *Toronto Star* that the COMER lawsuit is "by far the most serious and important case I've ever done.... It impacts the entire country in a profound way, right down to the bone of our economics and the history of the way we've maintained and lost, through illegal action, our independent monetary policy. It's huge."[1]

The Heart of the Matter

Galati has an astonishing workload, as well as family commitments, and he did not respond to my requests for an interview. Nonetheless, by utilizing the lawsuit's Statement of Claim and a presentation by Galati in 2012, it's possible to summarize the heart of the lawsuit.

The key issue is the government's abdication of its constitutional duty to enforce and apply the *Bank of Canada Act*, by which the BOC was set up to make interest-free loans as its statuary duty and responsibility.

As the lawsuit's Statement of Claim puts it, the government and the Minister of Finance "have abdicated their constitutional duty(ies) and handed them over to those international, private entities, whose interests, and directives, are placed above the interests of Canadians, and the primacy of the *Constitution of Canada*, not only with respect to its specific provisions, but also with respect to the underlying constitutional imperatives.... [S]ince 1974, there has been a gradual, but sure, slide into the reality that the Bank of Canada, and Canada's monetary and financial policy are, in fact, by and large, dictated by private foreign bank and financial interests, contrary to the *Act*."[2]

Further, the Claim states, "[N]o sovereign government such as Canada, under any circumstances, should borrow money from commercial banks, at interest, when it can, instead, borrow from its central bank interest-free, particularly when that central bank, unlike any other G8 nation, is publicly established, mandated, owned, and accountable to Parliament, and the Minister of Finance, and was created with that purpose as one of its main functions."[3]

As Murray Dobbin has written, "Galati argues that not only *may* the Bank of Canada lend interest-free to the government, it is obliged to."[4]

The Hon. Paul T. Hellyer puts it very succinctly: "Under our Constitution, Parliament has absolute authority over money and banking in Canada," he writes. "Private banks have no rights; they are only licencees which must obey rules set by Parliament."[5]

Interested readers can find the lawsuit's December 2011 Statement of Claim published in the COMER website's archival issue of *Economic Reform*, January 2012.

"Strange Blackout"

The *Toronto Star* once called Toronto-born COMER co-founder William Krehm "this violinist-turned-revolutionary-cum-journalist-turned-businessman," who met George Orwell during the Spanish Civil War, endured political imprisonment, retreated to Mexico where he ended up standing guard over Trotsky's body during the funeral, and who then landed a job with *Time Magazine*, covering revolutions in Latin America during World War II.[6] "But by 1947," wrote the *Toronto Star*, "with the Cold War heating up, his revolutionary past came back to haunt him. 'I ruffled some feathers,' he says, about his dispatches on American involvement in several coups in Latin America. He was fired by *Time*."[7]

Krehm returned to Toronto with his wife and son, and eventually ran a successful property management company until the 1980s, when he retired and took up writing about economics. Krehm started meeting with like-minded economics professors and practicing economists, and they decided to form the think tank in the late 1980s. "It was Bill [Krehm] and Dr. John Hotson at the University of Waterloo, and Harry Pope at Ryerson who were the key people" in getting COMER going, Ann Emmett told me. They had these "marvelous meetings and seminars" where people could learn about economic matters.

In particular, the economists were interested in the Bank of Canada. As Krehm wrote in 1997, Canadians had forgotten what the BOC had actually done for the country for 35 years. "That strange blackout of our national memory is due largely to a brilliantly organized world campaign of speculative finance to regain the hegemony it had lost due to its excesses in the twenties [1920s]," he wrote.[8]

That "blackout of our national memory" continues, with the help of the corporate media.

For example, in March 2012, then-federal Finance Minister Jim Flaherty released his austerity budget: chopping 19,200 public sector jobs, cutting federal programs by $5.2 billion per year, and raising the retirement age for millions of Canadians from 65 to 67. The explanation for the Harper cuts was a federal debt that had reached C$581 billion by 2011. On the very same day, the *Globe and Mail* published an online budget game that invited readers to try to balance the budget themselves, giving readers "a taste of the decision making involved."[9]

As *Web of Debt* author Ellen Brown noted in her blog, "Possibilities included slashing transfer payments for elderly benefits, retirement programs, health benefits, and education; cutting funding for transportation, national defense, economic development and foreign aid; and raising taxes. An article on the same page said, 'The government, in reality, doesn't have that many tools at its disposal to close a large budgetary deficit. It can either raise taxes or cut departmental program spending'."[10]

Overlooked by the game creators, as well as by the *Globe and Mail* itself, was the possibility of borrowing from the government's own Bank of Canada. Ellen Brown wrote, "It seems that no gamer, lawmaker or otherwise, was offered the opportunity to toy with the number one line item in the budget: interest to [private] creditors. A chart on the website of the Department of Finance Canada titled 'Where Your Tax Dollar Goes' shows interest payments [called 'servicing the debt'] to be 15% of the budget – more than health care, social security, and other transfer payments combined."[11]

Clearly, a massive share of the debt could be eliminated by borrowing from the government's own Bank of Canada, but on budget day 2012 readers of the *Globe and Mail* were told there were only two choices: raise taxes or cut government spending. It's hard not to see this as deliberate misinformation, especially given that the COMER lawsuit had been launched only a few months previous.

Power of the Banksters

The loss of public memory has been brutal. As Ellen Brown has written, governments and voters alike – not just in Canada, but around the world – "are convinced that the only alternatives for addressing the debt crisis are to raise taxes, slash [public] services, or sell off public assets. We have forgotten that there is another option: cut the debt through the use of publicly-owned banks that return the interest to public coffers."[12]

Just as Stephane Hessel powerfully reminded Europeans that France had nationalized its banks after World War II in order to fund renewal of the country on a more equitable basis, so members of COMER have doggedly persisted in not just maintaining their lawsuit, but in attempting to revive the national memory.

Recently, economist Michael Hudson recalled his experience in Canada in 1979 when he was writing on monetary issues for an institute. He noted: "At that time, the provinces of Canada were borrowing money from Switzerland and Germany because they could borrow it at much lower interest rates" than from other private lenders. "I said that this was going to be a disaster, and one that was completely unnecessary ... Why not have the central bank [BOC] simply create these dollars without having Swiss francs, without having Germany marks? It's unnecessary to have an intermediary. But the more thuggish banks, like the Bank of Nova Scotia [Scotiabank], said, 'Oh, that way's the road to serfdom.' It's not. Following the banks and the Austrian School of the banks' philosophy, that's the road to serfdom. That's the road to debt serfdom."[13] Right-wing Austrian economist Friedrich Hayek's best-known book is called *The Road to Serfdom*.

Hudson also told the interviewer that "my experience there [in Canada] was that the banks have a huge lobbying power over governments."[14] That lobbying power apparently hasn't diminished at all over the decades. The Justin Trudeau Liberals are now embracing trade deals like CETA and TPP which will prevent banking and monetary reform, not just in Canada but across the planet.

9. The EU Flaunts Its Undemocratic Tendencies

Who knows whether the hordes of Brits who voted for Brexit on June 23, 2016 were ignorant, manipulated louts, or savvy anti-globalists, or (more likely) a mixture of both. But at least one upshot of the resulting turmoil is that two of the pending trade deals – CETA and TTIP – are in some doubt. In that sense, the rest of us peasants owe a debt to the Brexiteers for (at least temporarily) throwing a monkey wrench into the works, as these trade deals promise to lock in extraordinary powers for multinational corporations..

Especially at risk in these trade deals are the efforts that are growing worldwide to take banking back into the public sector, whether through postal banking, state-owned banks like the Bank of North Dakota, public-interest banks like Sparkassen of Germany, or publicly-owned credit unions and central banks. Outraged by the 2008 bank bailouts, some countries (including Iceland and Switzerland) are seriously considering plans to remove the power to create money from private banks and return that power to their federal governments. As we shall see, the pending trade deals would undermine these goals.

As *Web of Debt* author Ellen Brown has written, "From our western perspective, we tend to forget that, globally, around 40 per cent of banks are already publicly owned, many of them concentrated in the BRIC economies, Brazil, Russia, India and China. Banking is not just a market good or service. It is a vital part of societal infrastructure, which properly belongs in the public sector. By taking banking back into the public sector, local governments could regain control of that very large slice (up to 40 per cent) of every public budget that currently goes to interest charged" by private banks for loans to governments.[1]

In terms of the negotiation process, the most advanced of the trade deals is CETA, the Comprehensive Economic and Trade Agreement between Canada and Europe. Just days after the Brexit vote, the EU bureaucrats – no doubt stung by this rejection of their authority – seemed intent on showing the world just how undemocratic they can be.

Stung by Brexit

On June 28, 2016 a German news agency reported that European Commission (EC) President Jean-Claude Juncker told EU leaders the Commission is planning to push through CETA without giving national parliaments any say in it.[2] According to the German press, Juncker argued that allowing national parliaments to vote on the agreement would "paralyze the process" and raise questions about the EU's "credibility." Juncker claimed that CETA "would fall within the exclusive competence of the EU executive" and therefore doesn't need to be ratified by national parliaments within the 28-nation bloc, sources in Brussels told the German news agency DPA.[3]

Most EU members, however, view CETA as a "mixed" agreement, meaning "that each country would have to push the deal through their parliaments," a process that could delay the deal by several years.[4] Juncker was reported as saying that he "personally couldn't care less" whether lawmakers get to vote on CETA.[5]

Millions of Canadians and Europeans have fought against CETA for years, at least since 2010 when some of the secret negotiating texts were leaked, but in September 2014 (during the reign of PM Stephen Harper) the CETA deal was signed without any public consultation whatsoever in Canada. The 2014 announcement was also the first time Canadians and Europeans (aside from corporate lobbyists) were allowed to see the official text, which had been kept secret during the years of negotiations.

The Canadian Target

The case for any big gains for Canadians under CETA has long been suspect. Canadian exports to the EU are quite modest. For example, in 2012 Canadian total exports worldwide amounted to about $463 billion, with only about $41 billion of those exports to the EU.[6]

But there are at least 42,000 U.S. branch-plant companies in Canada – the subsidiaries of multinationals – who would have much to gain from CETA (and the other trade deals), not just in terms of markets, but in terms of labour negotiations in Canada. These footloose multinationals can just pick up and move shop if they find a better deal (taxes, subsidies, wages and labour relations, regulations) elsewhere – making entire communities hostage to their demands.

As labour activist Sean Smith wrote in 2010, "Canadians need to learn that the CETA talks have nothing to do with giving Canadians a good alternative to American markets and forging closer ties with happy Swedes and Danes and other progressive Europeans. That mythical EU is disappearing faster than a Greek pension and is being replaced by a corporatist continent that thrives on things like Bulgaria's minimum wage of 97 Canadian cents an hour."[7]

As well, European corporations are "eager to get a piece of our Crown corporations being offered up as prizes (they have already mentioned postal services, public auto insurance, liquor boards and public utilities as being 'anti-competitive monopolies'). Corporations in the EU will profit hugely when these public services and utilities are privatized and sold to them [under CETA]."[8]

Another big Canadian prize under CETA is in the financial sector.

Financial Targets

In 2014, the COMER newsletter published a piece by Rick Tufts, who wrote that then-PM Stephen Harper "has inserted a clause in CETA ... that would permanently eliminate the right of the Bank of Canada to create money for the various levels of government in Canada, thus permanently securing the original change by the government and the Bank of Canada in 1974. This more than likely is a response to the efforts of COMER who have taken the government to court" to return to that mandate.[9]

Tufts' warning was confirmed by a major November 2014 report on CETA released by a collection of Canadian and European NGOs. The report stated: "CETA would give foreign investors more rights to challenge financial regulations [in Canada] than NAFTA, where they were mostly limited to a bank's (still wide-ranging) rights to transfer funds freely and to be protected from expropriation. CETA expands their rights to include highly elastic concepts such as fair and equitable treatment, which threatens to hamstring regulators charged with protecting consumers and the stability of the financial system in an emergency."[10]

It appears that foreign investors and bankers claiming "fair and equitable treatment" under CETA could target any lending (or even potential lending) by the Bank of Canada to the provinces and municipalities as cutting into their future private profits. They could likely sue the government(s) on that basis, using the Investor-State Dispute Settlement (ISDS) clause in CETA. "The risks to Canada of being sued by banks, insurers and holding companies will increase significantly with CETA. These risks are evident as speculative investors, backed by investment lawyers, are increasingly using investment arbitration to scavenge for profits by suing governments experiencing financial crises. EU investment stocks in Canada are significant in the financial sector, which would gain far-reaching litigation rights under CETA."[11]

So the EU's late June 2016 move to exclude national parliaments from CETA ratification and instead simply rubberstamp it on its own was quite a statement of the EC bureaucrats' disdain for democracy. Unfortunately, the Liberal government of Justin Trudeau has been cheering about all this.

The Plutocrat

In a July 3, 2016 interview with *The Globe and Mail*, Canada's International Trade Minister Chrystia Freeland enthused about what the EU is doing with CETA. "The British vote to exit the European Union has refocused Europe's attention on the need to send a message to the world that liberalized trade is the path to greater prosperity, Ms. Freeland said."[12] Readers may recall that Chrystia Freeland entered politics following the publication in 2013 of her book, *Plutocrats: The Rise of the New Global Super-Rich and the Fall of Everyone Else*. It was a title that likely sucked in lots of readers (including me). Instead, it was little more than a journalistic curtsy to the overlords. Indeed, Freeland has actually referred to "our imagined idea of a nefarious plutocracy," implying that any doubts we may have about the 1% are ludicrous and "imagined" whole cloth from our deranged musings.[13]

So we shouldn't be surprised that Freeland, in her new role as Canada's International Trade Minister, is thrilled about CETA and eager to boost it among her political peers. She told *The Globe and Mail* (July 3, 2016), "It is now just over a week since the Brexit vote and I've spoken to all our leading European Union partners," she said. "I can absolutely report to Canadians that support is strong and, if anything, there is a view now in the European Union that CETA has really taken on an important political symbolic significance ... I remain confident that CETA will be signed in the fall [2016] and will be ratified next year."[14] Freeland also explained that once the European Parliament approves CETA, "a great deal of the agreement would come into force immediately, more than 90 per cent," she said, "those portions deemed to be within the European Union's jurisdiction, those go into force right away."[15]

The Pushback

Reportedly, the pushback in Europe was immediate, with Germany, France, Austria, Belgium and the Netherlands expressing doubts about the deal and wanting their national parliaments to be involved in CETA ratification. On July 5, 2016 Germany news outlet *Deutsche Welle* reported that "Juncker appears to be backtracking," and would propose at a July 5 EC meeting that CETA would require "both the approval of the European parliament and national legislatures."[16]

The Globe and Mail reported on July 5 that Juncker's "new recommendation ... could call for applying those EU parts of the treaty while the ratification process [by national legislatures] is underway."[17] That would mean (as Freeland had earlier explained) more than 90% of CETA would be approved by the EU as part of its "jurisdiction" and needing no national legislative approvals. Such a process would make a mockery of democratic rights on both sides of the Atlantic.

And that appears to be exactly what is happening.

Following the July 5 EC meeting in Strasbourg, France, the CBC reported: "Legal opinions advanced by the [EC] commission suggest that most of the agreement – perhaps as much as 95 per cent – falls comfortably with the European Union's jurisdiction ... 'This is an agreement that Europe needs,' EU trade commissioner Cecilia Malmstrom said in a statement. 'The open issue of competence for such trade agreements will be for the European Court of Justice to clarify, in the near future. From a strict legal standpoint, the commission considers this agreement to fall under exclusive EU competence. However, the political situation in the council is clear, and we understand the need for proposing it as a 'mixed' agreement, in order to allow for a speedy signature'."[18]

A PR Stunt?

As it turns out, that consultation may be little more than a public relations stunt. While nations gear up to wrangle with the EU (in the European Court of Justice) over what parts of the CETA treaty fall within their jurisdiction, and what parts "fall under exclusive EU competence," the EC could approve 95 per cent of CETA before elected legislatures even vote.

The Council of Canadians warned (July 5, 2016): "One important concern to note, 'The commission may recommend provisionally applying the EU-parts of the Canada deal while full ratification is pending.' The French newspaper *Le Monde* has previously reported that even if CETA is deemed to be a 'mixed' agreement, the deal could enter into force 'provisionally' even before EU member state parliaments vote on it. It notes, 'If EU ministers agreed at the signing of the CETA on its provisional application, it could come into effect the following month. Such a decision would have serious implications. Symbolically, first because it would send the message that European governments finally [have] little regard for the views of parliamentarians and thus of European citizens strongly against the agreement'."[19]

After the July 5 EC meeting in Strasbourg, Council of Canadians National Chairperson Made Barlow stated, "Like many Canadians, Europeans are worried about CETA's attacks on democracy, its weakening of social and safety standards, its contribution to privatization and attacks on public services. After the Brexit vote, policy makers on both sides of the Atlantic would be better counseled to listen to voters, rather than pushing discredited [trade] solutions down people's throats."[20]

But on July 6, Canadian international trade lawyer Lawrence Herman, a senior fellow at the C.D. Howe Institute, told readers of his *Globe and Mail* op-ed that "there are important parts of CETA that can be put into operation now, whatever the final outcome of the ratification process" in Europe. He singled out "financial and banking regulations," saying that "the EU organs in Brussels have exclusive authority under various EU treaties."[21]

The implications of this are dire and threaten any attempts to reform monetary policy in Canada and Europe.

Bankster Cronyism

Global Justice Now director Nick Dearden has called CETA a "toxic deal" and says that the way the EC is acting "reinforces the widely held suspicion that the EU makes big decisions with harmful consequences for ordinary people with very little in the way of democratic process," he said. "Rather than take a step back and question why there is hostility to the EU, they try to speed up this awful trade deal."[22]

Then, in a brazen move that shocked much of Europe, news reports revealed in mid-July that Jose Manuel Barroso – former EC President (2004 – 2014) and Juncker's predecessor – had been appointed Chairman of Goldman Sachs International (to advise on post-Brexit issues), and that he had also been appointed to the Bilderberg Steering Committee, having attended Bilderberg in 2015 and 2016.[23] As PR optics go, the appointments couldn't have come at a worse time for the EU.

(The Chair of the Bilderberg Steering Committee, Henri de Castries, happens to be an Advisory Board Member of the think tank Focusing Capital on the Long Term, founded by CPPIB and McKinsey in 2013.)

By the end of August 2016, a coalition of German NGOs had launched a complaint with Germany's Constitutional Court, asking the judges to block provisional implementation of CETA on constitutional grounds.[24] As well, 3.5 million Europeans have signed a petition against CETA.[25] Doubling down to get CETA in place, during the September G20 meeting in China, PM Justin Trudeau met with Juncker and European Council president Donald Tusk to discuss CETA, while also pushing for the deal with G20 leaders.[26]

As opposition to the trade deal grows, the oligarchs predictably have a few tricks up their sleeves, including a back-up plan in the form of another (little-known) trade deal called TISA, the Trade In Services Agreement.

10. CETA: The "No Lawyers Left Behind" Treaty

As of July 2016, the Canada-EU trade deal called CETA (Comprehensive Economic and Trade Agreement) is being rammed down our throats on both sides of the Atlantic, and portions of it could come into effect as soon as November, according to the Council of Canadians. PM Justin Trudeau is scheduled to sign CETA in Brussels on October 27.

This draconian treaty – like TPP, TTIP and TISA – would give multinational corporations immense power to overrule elected local governments on numerous fronts. But one of its most controversial provisions is that it will allow for dozens more corporate lawsuits to be filed each year against the Canadian government (and European governments) under its investor-state dispute settlement (ISDS) mechanism.

The ISDS, first introduced in NAFTA, allows foreign corporations to sue governments over policy decisions or regulations that harm their future profits. For example, TransCanada Corporation is suing the U.S. government (under NAFTA) for more than $15 billion for failing to approve the Keystone XL tar sands pipeline, even though the company invested just $2.4 billion in the controversial project. With ISDS, there is no upper limit to how much money a company can claim in "lost future profits."

The year 2015 saw a record high of 70 new ISDS corporate lawsuits filed against countries under NAFTA and various bilateral treaties, raising concerns worldwide about ISDS and the ways corporations use it to bleed governments financially while putting a "chill" on any new regulations.

Current deals like CETA, TPP, TTIP, and TISA would open up huge vistas around the globe for ISDS lawsuits – which is one reason why the multinational corporate sector is pushing the deals so relentlessly.

ISDS "Rewrite"

Canada's International Trade Minister Chrystia Freeland is enthusiastically touting CETA and hastening its implementation. On July 3, 2016 she told the *Globe and Mail* that concerns about ISDS in CETA have been eased: "Ms. Freeland said those concerns were addressed after the treaty's investment chapter was rewritten to strengthen the right of governments to regulate in areas of the environment, labour standards, public services and a fairer arbitration process."[1]

In an op-ed for the same newspaper (July 8), Freeland and Cecilia Malmstrom (the EU's Trade Commissioner) asserted: "... we also know that governments need to be free to act in the interests of their citizens. That's why, in February, we created in our trade agreement a deeply reformed approach reinforcing the sovereign right to regulate, making investor arbitration procedures fairer, independent and more transparent."[2]

Far from any "deeply reformed approach," the rewritten chapter is little different from its predecessor, according to a March 2016 report from the Corporate Europe Observatory (CEO). The rewrite is basically a PR re-branding exercise, giving ISDS a new name: the Investment Court System (ICS). Otherwise, "the proposed 'new' ICS is ISDS back from the dead," Pia Eberhardt wrote in the report appropriately called *The Zombie ISDS*.[3]

The Council of Canadians calls the reforms "smoke and mirrors" and says the changes to the investment chapter "actually make [the provisions] worse. The reforms enshrine extra rights for foreign investors that everyone else – including domestic investors – don't have. They allow foreign corporations to circumvent a country's own courts, giving them special status to challenge laws that apply equally to everyone through a [private] court system exclusively for their use."[4]

The "Inner Mafia"

In November 2012, CEOs Pia Eberhardt and Cecilia Olivet of the Transnational Institute exposed this ISDS private court system in a report called *Profiting from Injustice*. They revealed that a "small club of international law firms, arbitrators and financial speculators are fuelling an investment arbitration boom that is costing taxpayers billions of dollars and preventing legislation in the public interest" across the planet.[5] They found a handful of legal firms "are actively encouraging corporate clients to sue governments" under investment treaties containing the ISDS clause, while "top arbitrators are using their influence to secure investor-friendly rules and sustain the flow of multi-million dollar lawsuits."

At the heart of this "secretive but burgeoning legal industry," they found an "inner mafia" of fifteen arbitrators who (as of 2012) had decided on 55% of all known ISDS disputes – earning millions in fees for themselves and billions in ISDS settlements for their corporate clients. That "inner mafia" includes three Canadian lawyers: Marc Lalonde, L. Yves Fortier, and Henry Alvarez.[6]

Profiting from Injustice also revealed that private investment funds are speculating on ISDS court cases: lending money to companies so they can sue governments, and then taking a percentage of the final financial award. Such a gamble can be very lucrative: in a recent ISDS lawsuit, a national government was ordered to pay a whopping $50 billion to the claimant.

As of January 2015, there had been 37 known ISDS claims against Canada under NAFTA, with settled awards to corporations totalling about US$341 million.[7] As well, Canada has spent over $65 million on ISDS court costs and legal fees – which can average $8 million per case – and still faces more than $2.6 billion in pending claims.[8]

Under CETA's rebranded ISDS, the three for-profit arbitrators (now to be called "judges") who decide each case would be drawn from a pool of lawyers and would be paid US$3,000 per day, on top of a monthly retainer fee of 2,000 euros per month. In addition, they can moonlight as lawyers with the very same corporations launching the lawsuits.

The CETA deal would allow for many more corporations to sue governments on both sides of the Atlantic.

CETA also for the first time prevents Canadian provinces and municipalities from favouring local contractors, so European companies will be vying for federal, provincial, and municipal procurement contracts worth more than $100 billion per year. Dozens of Canadian municipalities (including the Union of BC Municipalities) are officially opposed to CETA. Legal experts predict that lawsuits over lost contracts will mushroom in Canada, and likely in Europe as well.[9]

Think of CETA as the "no lawyers left behind" treaty.

"Illegal and Unconstitutional"

In 2012, the Canadian Union of Public Employees (CUPE) released a legal analysis of leaked negotiating texts showing CETA would "trump provincial powers over natural resources and public services" and "override areas of provincial jurisdiction set in the Constitution."[10]

After CETA was approved in principle in October 2013 by the Harper government, constitutional lawyer Rocco Galati stated publicly: "Your government has told you that we have a CETA with Europe but we don't know the details of it. We don't know what's in it. Have we gone back to the Middle Ages?"

Galati argues, "In the States, they cannot implement a treaty without passing it through Congress. In Canada, we pretend and fantasize and continue to invoke the 'Crown prerogative' of the executive [i.e, the Prime Minister] to sign treaties." But, Galati says, "There is no Crown prerogative left after the 1982 patriation of the Constitution." Therefore, any treaty "should have Parliamentary approval before the treaty has any effect, to ensure that it's reviewed for Constitutional conformity."[11]

In late September 2014, then PM Stephen Harper, European Commission Jose Manuel Barrosso, and European Council President Herman Van Rompoy signed a joint declaration marking the end of negotiations on CETA. That was the first time people in Canada and Europe were allowed to see the official text, although we were told that no changes to it would be allowed.

Just days after the signing, the *Globe and Mail* reported (September 30, 2014), "The CETA must still be approved by the Canadian Parliament and provinces and European parliaments," although it is "unclear whether all [Canadian] provinces and territories will hold votes in their legislatures, or whether some will approve the deal through regulation or other means."[12]

But Gus Van Harten, international investment law expert at Osgoode Hall Law School in Toronto, told me by email in July 2016 that CETA never was voted on by the Canadian Parliament or any provincial/territorial legislature. Van Harten stated: "Personally I think trade agreements of this magnitude should be voted on federally and in each province or territory, prior to Canada's ratification of the agreement, due to their broad-ranging implications for governments and legislatures."

Rocco Galati goes further, calling CETA "illegal and unconstitutional."

Back to the Middle Ages

Galati has explained: "The federal government cannot sign a treaty in which they sign and bind exclusive provincial and First Nation rights vis-a-vis other countries that they can't implement in Canada, but then have to compensate foreign countries and companies when they can't do business under the treaty."

An example is the pending C$250 million ISDS lawsuit filed by Lone Pine Resources (under NAFTA) after Quebec instituted a temporary moratorium against fracking.

CETA (like NAFTA) "puts the treaty above Canadian sovereignty," Galati says. "It puts the treaty above the Constitution, private interest over the Constitution. That's what's wrong with it."

As well, this situation sets up a framework in which "they're giving away the family store to their friends, in essence," Galati says, through the ISDS lawsuits that then are pursued. "My personal theory is this is just money going between friends in different countries," Galati has stated publicly.

That "theory" was largely confirmed by the *Profiting from Injustice* report which revealed the "inner mafia" of lawyers and law firms reaping vast sums from ISDS. The new report from CEO, *The Zombie ISDS*, states that the CETA investment rewrite raises "concerns that tribunals will be staffed with the same private lawyers who have until now driven the boom in investment arbitration."

While CETA would allow European companies to sue Canada under ISDS for "lost future profits," some 42,000 U.S. multinationals that have branch-plants in Canada could sue European governments through CETA – a kind of "back door" in case the equally controversial Transatlantic Trade and Investment Partnership (TTIP) between the U.S. and the EU collapses, as it well might under Brexit and popular opposition in both the U.S. and Europe.[13]

Assault on Democracy

On June 28, 2016 a German news agency reported that European Commission (EC) President Jean-Claude Juncker told EU leaders the Commission is planning to push CETA through without giving national parliaments any say in it. After pushback in Europe, Juncker appeared to be backtracking, recommending as of July 5 that CETA is a mixed treaty that would require "both the approval of the European parliament and national legislatures" in the 28-member EU bloc.

But the EC believes that 95% of CETA falls within EU jurisdiction and could be implemented immediately after the October 27, 2016 signing, leaving the other 5% of the deal to be voted on in European legislatures.

That process seems to have been planned for some time. In March 2016, Canada's chief negotiator, Steve Verheul told *iPolitics*, "After the agreement is approved by the European Parliament, the EU will pursue something called provisional application, which will allow them to put in place probably 95 per cent of the agreement. And then member [European] states could subsequently ratify, if that's required, over a period of time that would be of less concern to us."[14]

The 95% of CETA that the EC considers part of its "jurisdiction" includes the investment chapter with its ISDS "reforms".

Even worse, according to European trade analyst Felix Heilmann,

Article 30.8 of CETA states that countries "would be subject to corporate lawsuits even if they decide against CETA – for three whole years!"[15] *Le Monde* and Council of Canadians have also reported that even if CETA is rejected in Europe, "claims under the ISDS chapter would still be possible up to three years afterwards for investments made during the provisional period."[16]

Spinning CETA

On July 5, 2016 *The Globe and Mail* published an op-ed by Canadian business advisor Omar Allam, urging the private sector to "rally behind Ottawa" on CETA. "Our companies (especially our small-and mid-market firms) stand to benefit from CETA, which would open significant export and investment opportunities for Canadian companies to do business in and with Europe in a wide range of sectors," he wrote.[17]

But according to federal figures cited by the *Toronto Star* in 2014, "Of the more than one million small-to-medium sized businesses in Canada, just one in 30 does any exports," and those are to the U.S.[18] So one million Canadian companies aren't likely to benefit from CETA at all, and in fact, they could lose business, including procurement contracts, to European companies.

Some Canadian corporations that will benefit from CETA include Canadian multinationals (banks, mining, defense, oil and gas, aerospace, etc.) and the big law firms like Bennett Jones LLP, which is representing Lone Pine Resources in its ISDS dispute over Quebec's moratorium on fracking. John Baird, former Foreign Affairs Minister, joined Bennett Jones as senior advisor in May 2015.[19] Bennett Jones LLP advised the Harper government on CETA, and advertises "Investment Treaties and Disputes" as one of its legal services for corporate clients.[20]

Of course, words like "investments" are always slippery in the legal world. In one infamous recent ISDS case, a company invested $5 million in a "tourism" project in Libya, but claimed (and got) $900 million in "lost future profits," even though construction had never started.

11. The Potential of Postal Banking

For North Americans, it's surprising to learn that many countries have successful postal banking systems. France's Banque Postale, Italy's Poste Italiane, Switzerland's PostFinance, the Japan Post Bank, the Postal Savings Bank of China, the Kiwibank in New Zealand, are just a few of the publicly-owned systems that are thriving.

In February 2014, Canadian parliamentary news site *Blacklock's Reporter* revealed that Canada Post had spent almost four years researching, polling and conducting focus group studies into the viability of postal banking, and concluded that Canada Post "could profitably launch the largest banking network in the country."[1] Of the 811-page study released under access to information legislation, 701 pages were redacted. Nonetheless, the report did conclude that offering postal banking services would be a "win-win strategy."

The Canadian Union of Postal Workers (CUPW) has been trying valiantly to obtain the entire report. On July 19, 2016 CUPW's National President Mike Palecek wrote to Deepak Chopra, President and CEO of Canada Post: "For two years, we have requested an uncensored copy of Canada Post's postal banking work ... Our members and the people of this country can have no confidence in a management team that keeps such vital information secret. Canada Post is a crown corporation that belongs to ALL OF US. You, Mr. Chopra, have no right to keep this information from the public."[2]

Copies of the letter were sent to PM Justin Trudeau and Judy Foote, Minister of Public Services and Procurement, in hopes that the new regime in Ottawa would finally release the full report. A federal task force is reviewing Canada Post and deciding on its future, so it would be of great benefit to know what the internal study determined.

Despite the fact Canada Post had concluded that postal banking was a "proven money-maker," the Harper government not only hid the study but raised postal rates, cut postal services, and began the elimination of door-to-door postal delivery. As Ethan Cox wrote in the *Toronto Star*: "If our government is not acting in our best interests, as citizens and clients of Canada Post, whose interests are they upholding?"[3]

The Banking Lobby

The Canadian Bankers Association submitted a brief to the federal task force, stating that there's no need for postal banking and "no public policy objective or existing gap in the marketplace" that would justify Canada Post offering such services.[4] CUPW President Mike Palecek fired back, "We're not surprised that the big banks, which raked in a $35 billion profit last year by gouging Canadians with some of the highest fees in the world, would oppose a public banking option."[5]

Contrary to the lobbyists' claims that Canadians are already "well-served" by the big banks, CUPW counters that thousands of towns, villages and First Nations reserves across Canada have no bank, but many of them do have a post office that could provide financial and banking services. Over 600 Canadian municipalities have passed resolutions that support postal banking.[6]

As *rabble.ca*'s David J. Climenhaga reminds readers, Canada actually had a national postal banking system from 1868 until 1969, "when the commercial banking lobby managed to get it shut down."[7] But in subsequent years, banks and credit unions have been closing outlets in rural areas, while any new outlets that are opened tend to be located in wealthy urban centres. Now there at least two million Canadians across the country that have no banking services in their area, but they do have a postal outlet that could easily become a public bank offering basic services and "an alternative to predatory payday lenders."[8] CUPW wants the government review of Canada Post to recommend the addition of financial and banking services at Canada Post, or at a minimum, a task force to determine how to deliver new banking services through the postal outlets.

In the U.S., Ralph Nader wrote that commercial banks are "increasingly closing up shop in low-income areas," and he quoted findings from Bloomberg that showed from 2008 to 2013, banks have shut 1,826 branches across the U.S., with 93 per cent of the closings "in postal codes where the household income is below the national median." As Nader put it, "If you are living in a low-income neighborhood, just finding a bank is difficult" in the U.S.[9]

Climenhaga wrote that both Nader and Canada's postal workers "advocate the same sensible solution: the creation of a national postal banking system to serve all citizens ...The United States Postal Service [USPS], wrote Mr. Nader, 'could expand to include paycheque cashing, pre-paid debit cards, bill payments, ATMs, savings accounts and small dollar loans'."[10]

A 2013 report by John Anderson, "Why Canada Needs Postal Banking," released by the Canadian Centre for Policy Alternatives, revealed "the closure of 1,700 bank branches and hundreds of credit unions over the last two decades" across Canada.[11] Anderson argued that "Canada Post has a high trust factor among Canadians, and an already existing skilled and stable workforce of 68,000 employees, some of whom could easily be trained to handle financial services. Thus it would not mean starting from scratch [on postal banking], but rather building on what already exists."[12] Canada Post already provides some financial services such as postal money orders, domestic and international money transfers, prepaid Visa cards, and other financial transactions.

"Venal Class"

In the U.S., states such as Vermont, Arizona and Washington, and cities such as Philadelphia, Washington, D.C., San Francisco, Santa Fe, and Reading, Pa., have begun public banking initiatives. As Chris Hedges notes, "Public banks return economic power, and by extension political power, to the citizens. And because they are local they are possible ... We will have to take back power, which in a corporate state is financial power, from the venal class of speculators who hold us hostage. In open defiance we will have to build our own independent institutions. Of course the speculators will fight back. And they will fight dirty – they know the consequences of this revolt."[13]

On the postal banking front, one way they "fight dirty" is to create an artificial budget crisis for the postal service. In the U.S., *Labor Notes* writer Alexandra Bradbury reported that the USPS "would be in the black if not for an extreme 2006 law that requires the agency to pre-fund retiree health benefits 75 years in advance, before some of these future retirees are even born ... The resulting USPS budget deficit has created an opportunity for privatization advocates to hack away."[14]

Another way to "fight dirty" is through outright privatization of the post office, which is being advocated in Canada by Conservative leadership candidate Maxime Bernier. The Quebec MP is calling for dismantling of all government monopolies and handing them over to the private sector.[15] The Trudeau Liberals have said that privatization of Canada Post is not being considered, and during the election campaign Trudeau promised to stop the plan to end home delivery.

On August 10, 2016 *rabble.ca* reported that Canada Post's CEO Deepak Chopra, chosen by the previous Harper regime, "refused the new Liberal government's request to resign."[16] Two weeks later, however, the CBC reported that Chopra's "term has been renewed."[17]

Before his appointment, Chopra was an executive with Pitney Bowes, the largest private mail supply company in the world. As CUPW's Mike Palecek has pointed out, "They are also a company that specializes in picking up the pieces of privatized postal services." In 2013, "Pitney Bowes published a study urging the privatization of the United States Postal Service, and have been lobbying heavily to do exactly that ... [Chopra] was not hired to fix [Canada's] post office; he was hired to destroy it."[18]

Chopra's predecessor, Moya Greene, was also a privatization expert, overseeing the privatization of CN Rail before coming to Canada Post. But she then moved on to the Royal Mail in the UK in 2010 in order to lead its 2013 privatization. In October 2013 a public stock offering of shares vastly undervalued the Royal Mail, short-changing UK taxpayers. By November 2013, UK Members of Parliament were grilling the investment banks who handled the IPO: Goldman Sachs, UBS, JP Morgan, Citibank, Deutsche Bank and stockbroker Panmure Gordon.[19] The value assigned to Royal Mail "was largely set by salesmen from Goldman Sachs and UBS, in conjunction with the government and its adviser, the investment bank Lazard."[20]

It was a classic example of ripping off the taxpayers by selling the shares on the cheap and then watching the profits to the new owners rise and rise. By December 2013, the 70% privatised Royal Mail had "already rewarded its first investors with a nearly 80-per-cent return and its earnings are expected to grow substantially over the next two years."[21]

Community Power

During the summer of 2016, a coalition of Canadian groups put forward a creative vision for the future of Canada Post. *Delivering Community Power* suggests a range of services (in addition to postal banking) that could make Canada Post more central to communities across the country, while keeping the institution public.[22]

But on September 12, the federal four-person task force report, called "Canada Post in the Digital Age: Discussion Paper," was released, stating that postal banking would be unlikely to generate a profit. Moreover, the report states that "having a government entity competing in the financial sector would contravene Canada's trade agreements with other countries."[23] A decision about the future of Canada Post will be made by spring 2017.

In the meantime, the Trudeau Liberals are avidly in favour of trade deals that not only prevent postal banking, but could lead to the privatization of Canada Post itself.

12. More Crappy Trade Deals: TPP and TISA

The Trudeau government signed the TransPacific Partnership (TPP) agreement on February 5, 2016, and then launched "public consultations" on it two months later. The Standing Committee on International Trade (CIIT) road-show of Town Hall meetings started rolling across the country from west to east, with its inaugural hearing in Vancouver on April 18.

Meghan Sali, a digital rights specialist with OpenMedia, was one of only 12 individuals and organizations called to speak to CIIT in Vancouver. Sali later wrote: "It's an odd time to start consulting with Canadians on a broad scale, and it puts both the government and the public in an awkward position. The government is hamstrung because the move betrays the potentially insincere nature of the consultations – what's the point in consulting if it's already a done deal? And the public is presented with an impossible choice, because the only remedy we have left is to demand a wholesale rejection of the TPP."[1]

Sali added, "One of the biggest problems with the TPP is just how little time we've had to look at the text and see what is actually in the agreement. The details were kept secret for the entirely of the negotiations. From when the TPP was published on November 5, 2015, until it was signed on February 5, 2016, Canadian experts and the public had less than 90 days to assess the impact of this agreement."[2]

Nonetheless, it was obvious that much of the public had done its homework on TPP, and a groundswell against it was growing. By the time the event rolled into Toronto on June 15, people were fired up and ready.

NAFTA On Steroids

The TPP has been called "NAFTA on steroids," posing major impacts on the 12 signatory countries: Canada, the U.S., Mexico, Australia, Brunei, Chile, Japan, Malaysia, New Zealand, Peru, Singapore, and Vietnam.

The Toronto Town Hall was held in the auditorium of the Rotman School of Management, University of Toronto – a venue that can seat at least 500 – and the place was packed, filled with a great buzz of excitement as people waited to hear from The Honourable Chrystia Freeland, Minister of International Trade, and three panelists: Jerry Dias, National President of Unifor Trade Union; Dr. Michael Geist, University of Ottawa law professor and Canada Research Chair in Internet and E-commerce law; and Daniel Schwanen, Vice President of Research at the C.D. Howe Institute. The moderator was Dr. Walid Hejazi, Associate Professor of International Business at the Rotman School.

In introducing Freeland, Hejazi usefully did some unprompted name-dropping: commenting on "how well-connected she is," having "brought Larry Summers" to the Rotman School recently. Up until that point, many may not have known that Larry Summers is both a mentor and a friend of Freeland.

Described as "in listening mode," Freeland said very little during the Town Hall. The federal government has to decide whether or not to ratify TPP by November 2017, although some say the U.S. is intent on ratifying it during the "lame duck" session after the presidential election.

By far the most popular speaker at the Toronto Town Hall was Jerry Dias, who called TPP "a total disaster" that "gives investors more rights than governments," and who predicted that "the dairy industry is going to get slaughtered" by TPP. Dr. Michael Geist called TPP "a bad deal that should be renegotiated or rejected," especially because of the ISDS mechanism in the deal. Even Dan Schwanen of the C.D. Howe Institute seemed tepid, saying the TPP would generate more jobs for Canada, but "is it huge? No."

After about fifteen minutes, the microphones were turned over to the audience to raise questions. This format seemed different from the hearing in Vancouver, although no explanation for the change was given. But neither Freeland nor anyone on the panel would be answering the questions – much to the disappointment of many – although a scribe for Freeland was diligently taking detailed notes. One audience member noted pointedly, "Are we just here to vent, or is there actually a possibility that we won't sign the TPP?" Another said, "This process is a bit demeaning. I almost feel like a serf pleading" for my rights.

Nonetheless, at least 100 audience members raised important questions about TPP – its affects on drug prices, farming, democracy, corporate power, Crown corporations, environmental regulations, local jobs, etc. By my count, only two people expressed support for TPP. Otherwise, the opposition to it was palpable, as expressed in one comment that got a huge round of applause: "If TPP is ratified by the Liberal government, it should be the last Liberal government for generations."

After about two hours, the event ended, with Freeland saying, "There is no rush on these consultations. No countries have yet ratified" the TPP. While many at the Town Hall were clearly knowledgeable, I noticed that only two people – COMER's Ann Emmett and Paul Hellyer – raised questions specifically about the trade deal's impact on monetary and financial matters.

There's much in TPP to raise such concerns.

Impacts on the Financial Sector

The website *exposethetpp.org* has summarised those impacts as follows: "The TPP would provide big banks with a backdoor means of rolling back efforts to re-regulate Wall Street in the wake of the global economic crisis. The deal would require domestic law [in all 12] signatory countries to conform to the now-rejected model of extreme deregulation that caused the crisis. The TPP would forbid countries from banning particularly risky financial products, such as the toxic derivatives that led to the $183 billion government bailout of AIG."[3] The AIG bailout was just one of the bailouts that saw trillions in taxpayer dollars handed to the perpetrators of financial collapse.

"The TPP would threaten the use of 'firewalls' – policies that are employed to stop the spread of risk between different types of financial institutions and products." While many in the United States have called for a reinstatement of the *Glass-Steagall Act*, "the TPP would bar such reform."[4] As we have seen, the late 1990s changes to the WTO's *Financial Services Agreement* forcefully pried open the banking sectors in some 156 countries. The TPP would prevent a dozen of those countries (including Canada, the U.S., and Mexico) from creating any such "firewall" to close the door on toxic financial products.

"The TPP would ban capital controls, an essential policy tool to control destabilizing flows of speculative money. Even the International Monetary Fund (IMF) has recently endorsed capital controls as legitimate for mitigating or preventing financial crises."[5] So-called "hot money" can flow suddenly into (or out of) a country, destabilizing the economy, usually for political purposes. As we'll see, Iceland used capital controls to good effect in restoring its economy, but the TPP would now prevent such action.

"The TPP would also prohibit taxes on Wall Street speculation. That means that there would be no hope of passing proposals like a Robin Hood Tax, which would impose a tiny tax on Wall Street transactions to tamp down speculation-fueled volatility while generating hundreds of billions of dollars' worth of revenue for social, health, or environmental causes."[6] Dozens of countries have been designing such a financial transactions tax.

"The TPP would empower financial firms to directly attack these government policies in foreign tribunals, and demand taxpayer compensation for policies they claim undermine their expected future profits."[7] The ISDS mechanism would be used to sue governments for potentially billions if they restrict private banking in any way. That alone would put a "chill" on such efforts. On September 7, 2016 more than 200 American law and economics professors signed a letter to Congress members urging them to reject TPP and other trade deals that include ISDS.

A "Receptive Ear"

According to the Public Banking Institute, many commentators "have speculated that the [TPP] agreement poses an immediate, long-term threat to publicly owned banks like the Bank of North Dakota. The rationale for this concern is that public banks are 'state-owned enterprises' that are seen as a barrier to private profits – something against which the TPP would throw considerable barriers."[8]

Financial analyst Sam Knight has argued that, under the terms of the TPP "foreign bankers could claim that [a publicly owned] bank stops them from lending to commercial banks," thereby depriving them of profits. Others have suggested that the TPP "would consider public banks to have unfair advantages and therefore violate free trade."[9]

The Public Banking Institute notes: "Given the tendency of trade negotiators to view banks as profit-making businesses [rather than as utilities] and to argue that state-owned enterprises should be evaluated through the criteria of pure 'commercial considerations,' there is understandable suspicion that passage of the TPP will significantly complicate the implementation and existence of public banks."[10]

The U.S. financial sector has spent millions lobbying for the TPP, hoping not just to gain access to more customers and investors in developing markets, but also to break down barriers to profits across the whole financial sector. These lobbyists have had a receptive ear in Michael Froman, the chief negotiator at the Office of the U.S. Trade Representative (USTR).[11] Froman is a former executive at Citigroup, as well as the former chief of staff at the U.S. Treasury Department, and he is said to have been 'instrumental' in the late 1990s repeal of *Glass-Steagall*.[12]

In May 2016, emails obtained through a Freedom of Information request by the U.S. non-governmental organization Rootstrikers showed USTR Froman discussing the TPP with Goldman Sachs lobbyists. As *commondreams* reported, a series of emails released by Rootstrikers "show what activists describe as 'collusion' between [USTR] Michael Froman and Wall Street executives to push for the passage [of] the controversial Trans-Pacific Partnership." The emails "include a message to Froman from a managing director at Goldman Sachs urging him to push for 'robust commitments' on Investor-State Dispute Settlement (ISDS) provisions ... 'I wanted to underscore how important it is for the financial services industry to get robust commitments on ISDS in the agreement... denying our industry the same rights as enjoyed by every other sector would be terribly unfortunate,' the email states."[13]

Froman responded "that he would assign a staff member to be in contact with Goldman Sach's lobbying team, and that he would 'welcome the chance to pick your brain' on the equally controversial Transatlantic Trade and Investment Partnership (TTIP)."[14] Froman was also involved in weakening the EU's fuel quality standards on behalf of U.S. refiners of tar sands crude.

Attack on Crown Corporations

Secret 2013 TPP briefing notes obtained and released by WikiLeaks in 2015 revealed that Crown corporations in Canada – such as the CBC and the Canada Post – could be required to operate solely for profit under the terms of TPP. As the *Huffington Post* reported, the briefing notes also raise questions "about the extent to which Canada will be able to continue using taxpayers' money to fund Crown corporations, such as the $1 billion annual subsidy to the CBC."[15]

Jane Kelsey, a law professor at the University of Auckland, analysed the TPP documents for WikiLeaks. According to the *Huffington Post*, "Kelsey says the U.S. is pushing to have state-owned businesses covered under the TPP's investor-state dispute mechanism. This would mean that foreign entities could sue the government of Canada for subsidizing a Crown corporation if that foreign entity can prove it's at a competitive disadvantage because of those subsidies. She describes the proposal as 'intrinsically problematic.' State-owned corporations 'are almost always state-owned because they have functions other than those that are merely commercial, such as guaranteed access to important services' or social and cultural functions, Kelsey wrote. She also suggested that the rationale for the existence of state-owned enterprises would be undermined by the TPP rules. 'Once SOEs and private firms are "competitively neutral," the advocates of privatization will say there is no justification for retaining state ownership because the private sector can bring efficiency gains, choice and competition to the provision of the public service'."[16]

While these 2013 briefing notes reportedly stated that negotiating countries could choose to protect the status of their Crown corporations, it is not known whether such flexibility for exceptions has been retained as of 2016. A legal opinion obtained by the Canadian Union of Postal Workers (CUPW) suggested that "it is not unreasonable to regard the TPP as a threat to the future of Canada Post." In negotiating the TPP, the Harper government did not protect postal services, while Japan and Singapore did. This failure to protect Canada Post "raises the spectre" of an ISDS claim buttressed by TPP provisions.[17]

TISA: The Backup Deal

In addition to CETA, TTIP, and TPP, there is a fourth pending agreement that seems to be the back-up agreement in case the other agreements fail. It's a clever strategy, because while millions are aware of the other deals, few even know about TISA (Trade In Services Agreement). This pending agreement is even more draconian than the others, with negotiations expected to conclude by December 2016.

TISA was dreamed up by the Global Services Coalition, whose members include Citigroup, JP Morgan Chase, MetLife, Prudential, Verizon, and Wal-Mart.[18]

TISA involves 50 countries, including every advanced economy except the BRICS (Brazil, Russia, India, China, and South Africa). TISA is being negotiated in secret, with the unelected and unaccountable European Commission representing the 28 EU countries. Other countries negotiating TISA include Australia, Canada, Chile, Colombia, Costa Rica, Hong Kong, Iceland, Israel, Japan, Liechtenstein, Mexico, New Zealand, Pakistan, Panama, Paraguay, Peru, South Korea, Switzerland, Taiwan, Turkey, and the United States.

Nick Dearden, director of UK-based Global Justice Now (GJN), calls TISA "a massive, super-privatization deal covering everything from finance to education." TISA focuses on services, not goods, and primarily allows multinationals to provide services across national borders by turning public services into commodities. A GJN report states, "TISA considers all regulations to be trade barriers. This means that it has serious consequences for ... areas like labor rights, banking regulation and whether public services like electricity and water [and healthcare] are run for the benefit of the people or by profit-making multinational companies."[19]

A report by Public Services International has warned that TISA puts at risk public services such as healthcare, broadcasting, water and wastewater services, public transit and transport.[20]

According to Ellen Brown, TISA would lock the current financial system in place "so that there was no way to return money and banking to the service of the people – even if the current private [banking] model ended in disaster."[21] Recalling the WTO's Financial Services Agreement of the late 1990s – which forced countries around the world to open their banking systems to "liberalization" – TISA would prevent those banks from reforming.

TISA would also prevent the dismantling of privatizations in other sectors.

Undoing Privatizations

Many communities worldwide are recognizing the hazards of privatization of public assets and services and are attempting to return them to the public sector. After highly negative experiences under profit-driven privatization of water systems, electricity systems, waste management systems, transit systems, etc., many countries are moving to take those systems back into public hands. This is called "re-municipalization" because the reversals typically occur at the municipal level.

In 2015, the Netherlands-based Transnational Institute published a report showing that since the year 2000, there have been 235 cases across 37 countries where communities have taken back their water and sanitation systems, after privatization proved to be an economic disaster. At least 58 of those cases of remunicipalization occurred in the U.S., where contracts with water corporations such as Severn Trent and Veolia Water North America were cancelled by local authorities.[22]

TISA threatens remunicipalization, or any reversals of previous privatization of public services. The Transnational Institute has noted, "TISA will make it impossible for governments to reverse privatization or decrease the influence of the private sector. Governments will only be able to choose to maintain privatized services as they are or to extend liberalizations."[23] Similarly, Public Services International warns that TISA "would lock in current levels of services liberalization in each country, effectively banning any moves from a market-based to a state-based provision of public services."[24] As Brown writes, "That means we can forget about turning banking and credit services into public utilities. TISA is a one way street. Industries once privatized remain privatized."[25]

Tying the Hands of the State

On May 25, 2016 WikiLeaks released several chapters of the secret TISA negotiations, including the financial services annex. Writer Pete Dolack analyzed and summarized these latest TISA leaks, stating: "If TISA were to go into effect, regulation of the financial industry would be effectively prohibited, privatisations would be accelerated and the social security system would potentially be at risk of privatisation or elimination."[26]

The financial services annex of TISA "specifically references central banks, the social security system and public retirement systems. It is unclear how these would be affected, but it is possible that TISA could be interpreted to mean that no public or other democratic check would be allowed on central banks and that public systems such as Social Security might be judged to be illegally 'competing' with private financial enterprises. Financiers around the world would dearly love to get their hands on social security systems, a privatization that would lead to disaster, as has already been the case with Chile, also a TISA participant. Chileans retiring in 2005 received less than half of what they would have received had they been in the old government system."[27]

TISA would also curtail any government's attempts to hold a corporation financially responsible for an environmental disaster such as an oil spill. Dolack notes: "Environmental rules, even requiring performance bonds as insurance against, for example, oil spills, would be at risk of being declared unfair 'burdens' that don't meet the test of being necessary" to ensure quality of service.[28] As well, GJN's Nick Dearden writes that "some countries are pushing clauses in TISA which would prevent signatories introducing laws to favor renewable energy over fossil fuels."[29]

Dolack called TISA "a direct threat to what democracy is left to us. It promises a global dictatorship that in theory raises the level of corporations to the level of national governments but in reality raises them above governments because only corporations have the right to sue ... We ignore these naked power grabs at our collective peril."[30]

Indeed, a Global Justice Now report states that under TISA, "General elections will become increasingly pointless" – regardless of the outcome, "government's hands will be tied because TISA is an international agreement which has precedence" over national law.[31]

Illegal Deals?

A UN legal expert has scrutinized all four pending 'trade' deals and has found that, in terms of international law, all could be illegal because they trump human rights treaty obligations. Alfred de Zayas, the UN's Independent Expert on the Promotion of a Democratic and Equitable International Order, in 2016 released his findings on TPP, TTIP, TISA and CETA and condemned all of them, saying: "Trade deals prepared and negotiated in secret, excluding key stakeholders such as labour unions, consumer associations, health professionals, environmental experts and now parliaments, have zero democratic legitimacy."[32] With regard to TPP specifically, Mr. De Zayas has written, "Should the TPP ever enter into force, its compatibility with international law should be challenged before the International Court of Justice."[33] As Eric Zuesse reported, the UN expert "further damningly noted that, 'Disfranchising the public from participating in this important debate is undemocratic and manifests a profound disregard'" for the people.[34]

We're supposed to be little more than a collective cash-cow, bailing out the banksters and going along with their plans to disenfranchise us even further through these trade deals.

13. Hillary, Larry & Dominic: More Looting Opportunities

It's time for some high-level gossip involving the elites orchestrating our future.

In June 2016, *The Intercept* published an important article that undercut the anti-Wall Street rhetoric that has been coming from presidential candidates Donald Trump and Hillary Clinton during the campaign. Zaid Jilani wrote, "The head of the largest derivatives marketplace in the world, CME Group, told an audience at a financial industry conference that it doesn't matter if Hillary Clinton or Donald Trump becomes president because both understand the industry and are only criticizing it during the campaign for political reasons."[1]

CME Group Executive Chairman Terry Duffy, speaking at the Sandler O'Neill Global Exchange and Brokerage Conference on June 9, said: "I don't care if it's Donald Trump or Hillary Clinton ... I care who's around Donald Trump or Hillary Clinton, who's in the administration, who is helping them make the tough decisions to keep America on top, that's to me what's critically important."[2]

Duffy added, "So I think either way, what's important is the United States keep its status as the financial services leader. I think both of those two individuals understand that," he said, despite "any rhetoric you hear during the primary season."[3]

Both Trump and Clinton have taken swipes at Wall Street, but apparently it's all for show – like Obama's 2008 declaration that he would renegotiate NAFTA if elected, only to turn into the biggest advocate for so-called free trade in presidential history.

Reputational Damage

CME Group's Terry Duffy has defended the derivatives market on Capitol Hill, and in 2013 he wrote an op-ed for the *Wall Street Journal*, stating that "Wall Street has suffered reputational damage, thanks to a few bad actors."[4] It's a laughable moment – that "few bad actors" bit – but Duffy was undaunted: "I'm concerned that those of us in financial services have forgotten who we serve – and that the public knows it." He called out those "Wall Streeters" who "too easily slip into regarding their work as a kind of money-making game divorced from the concerns of Main Street."[5]

Duffy's op-ed caught the eye of Hillary Clinton. According to *The Intercept*, "Clinton had kind words for Duffy during an economic address she gave in July 2015. 'I think we should listen to Terry Duffy,' she said."[6]

So everybody's concerned about Main Street these days, or pretending to be concerned about Main Street. And in the U.S., a presidential election appears to be riding on just whose performance is most convincing. But for financial titans like CME Group's Terry Duffy, and likely many others, what really matters is who is picked for key administration posts.

If Clinton is elected, one person who might be in her administration is BlackRock's Larry Fink ... or at least that's been the financial gossip of late.

The Gossip

Fox Business News (of course!) seems to have started the gossip back in 2014 with a lengthy piece about how Fink "believes his career is incomplete unless he achieves the one goal that has eluded him for years – a presidential appointment to become U.S. Treasury Secretary." The piece noted that "Fink has told friends he would like to end his career in much the same way former Goldman chief Robert Rubin had, by shaping economic policy as Treasury Secretary," and Hillary Clinton might be his chance.[7]

One major sign that he's angling for the job, sources told Fox Business News, is "his October 2013 appointment of Democratic political operative and Hillary Clinton confidant Cheryl Mills to the BlackRock board of directors."[8] Mills was chief of staff to Secretary of State Clinton during Obama's first term, and she served in the administration of President Bill Clinton.

The gossip died down for a time, but then in late December 2015, *occupy.com* posted a lengthy piece stating that "Fink has been touted as a possible Treasury Secretary, the likelihood of which may increase if Clinton becomes president. Indeed, Fink, a longtime Democrat, would be perfectly suited to such a position as the 'top consigliere' of Wall Street in Washington, Suzanna Andrews writes in *Vanity Fair*, 'and the leading member of the country's financial oligarchy'."[9]

In late January 2016, Fink sent out his annual letter to top business leaders, urging them to resist "short-termism." Financial analysts at CNN noticed that the word "short-termism" is often used by Clinton on the campaign trail, where she also vows to "put an end to quarterly capitalism." They compared Fink's letter with Clinton's speeches, concluding that the "prominent Wall Street CEO sounds a lot like Hillary Clinton" and "may be positioning himself as a possible Treasury Secretary if Clinton wins the White House."[10]

Fortune picked up the story, showing how Fink's letter to CEOs "mirrors" Clinton, while "Clinton has echoed Fink's views on short-termism.[11] Then *The Intercept* joined the gossipy chorus, with Fink now said to be "poised to take over" at Treasury. David Dayen wrote, "Goldman Sachs paid Hillary Clinton $675,000 for three speeches, but an even bigger Wall Street player stands ready to mold and enact her economic and financial policy if she becomes president," with Fink's "ready-made team [at BlackRock] available for a move from Wall Street to Washington."[12] But the "most telling hire" at BlackRock is Cheryl Mills - Clinton's chief of staff at the State Department, deputy White House counsel during the Bill Clinton administration, and board member of the Clinton Foundation.[13]

Dayen noted that Fink's "priorities appear to be so in sync with Clinton's that it's not entirely clear who shares whose agenda." He noted that Clinton has mirrored Fink's "short-termism" language "to such a degree that the New York Times' Andrew Ross Sorkin suggested that Clinton 'could have been channeling Laurence D. Fink'."[14]

But as we know, it was McKinsey's Dominic Barton who in 2011 wrote the influential *Harvard Business Review* piece on the downside of "short-termism" and the need for capital to think long-term and beyond "quarterly capitalism." So Clinton may be channeling Larry Fink, but Larry Fink is channeling Dominic Barton.

That's important to know for a variety of reasons, including the fact that if Clinton becomes U.S. president, the predominant economic viewpoint on both sides of the Canada/U.S. border would be that of McKinsey & Company. Recalling Dominic Barton's prominent role with Larry Fink in the Focusing Capital for the Long Term think tank, these two players control vast financial assets, especially pension funds.

A "Looting Opportunity"

According to *The Intercept,* Larry Fink "opposes efforts to reinstitute the *Glass-Steagall* firewall between investment and commercial banks, as does Clinton ... Fink has also promoted the privatization of Social Security," noting that "Fink owes his initial backing at BlackRock to Pete Peterson, the former commerce secretary who has been at the forefront of the campaign to cut or privatize Social Security. [Fink] sat on the steering committee of the Campaign to Fix the Debt, a stalking horse for Peterson's ideas."[15] McKinsey & Company director Lenny Mendonca was involved in the same Campaign to Fix the Debt, along with CEOs from Bank of America, Goldman Sachs and other financial titans.

While Clinton has pledged not to cut or privatize Social Security benefits, Yves Smith (a writer for the website *nakedcapitalism.com*) recalls that Bill Clinton "was ready to privatize Social Security, but l'affaire Monica intervened. Ordinary Americans need to thank her for her service, in both senses of the word."[16]

Moreover, Smith notes, "Privatizing Social Security is another big business looting opportunity. Social Security is extraordinarily efficient from an administrative standpoint," while private accounts have "much greater costs of running them. And that's why Wall Street salivates over the idea of privatizing Social Security" because of high fees to advisors; "so the more they can do to get policymakers to drive assets in that direction, the more big financiers will make."[17]

In Canada, the *National Post's* Andrew Coyne is advocating a similar move regarding CPP contributions: diverting them "into personal retirement savings accounts in the name of every one of the CPP's 18 million beneficiaries – rather like RRSPs, only mandatory. These accounts would be the legal property of each beneficiary, to be invested at their direction. I make no claim to novelty for this idea: it's how public pensions are managed in Australia and Chile," Coyne wrote.[18]

It's also how private pensions – 401(k) and IRAs – are managed in the U.S., leading to the draining of people's retirement savings and cumulative losses of some $17 billion per year because of what's known as "the retirement advice loopholes." Advisers are supposed to put their clients' best interest first, but loopholes in the U.S. rules allow advisers to recommend retirement investments that pay lucrative commissions to themselves, while exposing the client to excessive costs and fees, poor performance, and even unnecessary risk.[19] As California Congresswoman Maxine Waters stated in October 2015, the loopholes "encourage advisers to, for example, push a 70-year-old retiree to invest more of her savings in a stock fund, rather than a less risky short term bond fund, simply because the adviser receives 150% more for making the riskier recommendation."[20]

Coyne doesn't explain that private financial advisors would make a killing on fees for their advice to those 18 million Canadian souls seeking to personally invest their mandatory retirement savings. In the U.S., the Department of Labor has been trying for years to close those advice loopholes, but it has been blocked repeatedly by lobbying from organizations like the Insured Retirement Institute – whose board of directors includes executives from BlackRock, and the Bank of America Merrill Lynch.[21]

More Channeling

In June 2016 on the campaign trail, Clinton continued railing against "short-termism" and she told *Business Insider* that she is "deeply distressed about quarterly capitalism because I think it is causing businesses to make decisions that are not helping the long-term profitability of American corporations or the success of our economy."[22] At a speech in Raleigh on June 22, Clinton focused on the economy and stated that "the heart of my plan will be the biggest investment in American infrastructure in decades, including establishing an infrastructure bank that will bring private sector dollars off the sidelines and put them to work here."[23]

Later Clinton unveiled a $300 billion five-year plan for federal infrastructure investment, and an additional government-funded $25 billion infrastructure bank – the intention of which, she said in August, is to "get private funds off the sidelines" and unlock $250 billion in private sector spending.[24]

The plans suggest that if Clinton is elected President, appointing Larry Fink as Treasury Secretary wouldn't even be necessary, aside from enacting a mere formality. Clinton has already drunk the Fink/Barton/McKinsey Kool-Aid, and the privatization bandwagon is set to roll out in a big way again in the U.S. too.

In August, after Clinton named her transition team (to choose her policy priorities, cabinet members and top staff), one analyst identified the team's economic priorities as pro-TPP, pro-austerity, and pro-privatization - including Social Security.[25]

For almost a decade, private investment firms such as Goldman Sachs, Morgan Stanley, Global Infrastructure Partners (a joint venture between Credit Suisse Group and General Electric), the Carlyle Group, and Kohlberg Kravis Roberts & Co. have been amassing huge dedicated funds for buying up and investing in infrastructure.[26] Canadian firms Brookfield Asset Management, Borealis Infrastructure and the pension funds (like the other members of the Global Infrastructure Investor Association) are also positioned for large U.S. infrastructure investments and asset recycling.[27]

In its April 2015 report called *Infrastructure Rising*, BlackRock complained that the U.S. is way behind on implementing P3s. "In 2014, only six PPP transactions closed in the U.S, compared with 18 in Canada," the company sniffed, while Australia is "an infrastructure trailblazer," and the UK "has been a rich source for core assets."[28]

Indeed, since the 1979 election of Margaret Thatcher (fan of Friedrich Hayek), a short list of public assets that have been privatized includes British Petroleum, British Aerospace, Associated British Ports, British Telecom, British Gas, British Airways, British Steel, 10 regional water agencies, the National grid and 12 regional electricity distribution firms, British Rail, the Royal Mail, and on and on.[29]

But as *The Tyee's* Mitchell Anderson noted in a brilliant article: "Thirty-five years after [Thatcher] swept to power as British prime minister, it is ironic that socialist Norway now has $830 billion in the bank and enjoys fully funded social programs ... Meanwhile the UK is enduring another round of wrenching austerity and owes over 1.3 trillion pounds – about US$1.2 trillion" in debt.[30]

Shock Therapy

Hillary Clinton has said that her husband would be her "Economics Czar." The Bill Clinton administration privatized some federal assets, including the Alaska Power Administration, the Elk Hills Naval Petroleum Reserve, the U.S. Enrichment Corporation, and Intelsat. Now, with a new administration coming into the White House, the privateers have their eye on more federal assets, including the U.S. Postal Service, Amtrak, the air traffic control system, water utilities, federal electricity infrastructure, interstate highways, bridges, seaports, airports, and even federal lands – including national parks.[31] Interior Secretary Sally Jewell has warned that public lands, including parks, risk "being sold off for a short-term gain."[32]

As economist Michael Hudson told Chris Hedges in a 2016 interview, "Well you can look at the future [of the U.S.] as what's happening in Greece, what happened in Russia after their traumatic shock therapy [in the early 1990s.] America's in for shock therapy, no matter who wins [the presidential] race," leading to "a rollback to feudalism."[33]

With governments already in hock to the overlords, selling such assets off in order to build new "toll-booth" infrastructure would complete the dream of the Ayn Rand enthusiasts, Milton Friedman disciples, and billionaires who view governments as their wholly-owned subsidiaries. Chris Hedges and Michael Hudson have starkly predicted the outcome: the U.S. will become "a nation of sharecroppers."[34]

Obviously, the financial oligarchy is moving fast, and so are others poised to profit from asset recycling, P3s, and the new federal infrastructure banks proposed for the U.S. and Canada. In mid-September 2016, CPPIB's Mark Jenkins left to take a senior leadership role at the Carlyle Group, the U.S. titan with billions of investor dollars.[35]

In a move timed for immediately after the U.S. federal election, BlackRock is hosting a private summit in Toronto on November 14, 2016 for "a select group of major international investors" with trillions of dollars in assets. They will be meeting with PM Justin Trudeau, Finance Minister Bill Morneau, Infrastructure Minister Amarjeet Sohi and other federal officials.[36] According to the *Toronto Star*, Trudeau will provide "an overview of the government's policy priorities, including 'a more innovative and cleaner' natural resources sector and a growing list of 'opportunities' for public-private partnerships in infrastructure, one federal source said."[37]

Pending the creation of a Canada Infrastructure Bank, "Justin Trudeau will tell BlackRock's guests that for now the window opens into his office. You want to invest in Canada? Call the PMO. 'That's a signal that hasn't been sent in a long time,' one official said."[38]

Whether or not the Canadian public will also be informed about these "policy priorities" and P3 "opportunities" being shared with Black-Rock's private guests is not clear. As we go to press, Minister Sohi's office has not responded to my requests for information, including the name of that banker from Bank of America Merrill Lynch advising on a CIB, the name of the report written by that banker, the date of the report's release, or how to obtain the report.

So I seriously doubt they'll tell us anything about BlackRock's private party with our elected officials.

14. Bilderberg & "The Wake Behind the Shark Fin"

When Bank of Canada Governor Stephen Poloz insisted in mid-April 2016 that the Federal Finance Minister "is not my boss," he may have been revealing more than he realized. Poloz was an invited guest at the 2014 Bilderberg meeting in Copenhagen, where he was able to hobnob with the top echelon of financial elite, including Robert Rubin and Larry Summers (guests that year) and the usual banksters (Goldman Sachs, Barclay's, HSBC, Lazard), CEOs (Royal Dutch Shell, ExxonMobil, General Electric, Siemens, etc.), and think tankers that flock to the secret conclave every year.

At Bilderberg 2014, Poloz would have mingled with five other Canadians, including Heather Munroe-Blum who, at the time, was still associated with McGill University.

By 2015, when Bilderberg met in Austria, Poloz wasn't there but Munroe-Blum was back. By then she had become Chair of the Canada Pension Plan Investment Board (CPPIB). At Bilderberg 2015, there were interesting guests for Munroe-Blum to meet with, including Philipp Hildebrande (Vice Chair of BlackRock), David McKay (President and CEO of the Royal Bank of Canada), and *National Post* columnist Andrew Coyne. Did they talk about public pension privatization and "asset recycling"? They're not saying, and we'll never know. But why else would those four have been invited in that particular year?

Less than a year later, Coyne wrote that federal money for spending on infrastructure would have to come from "three alternatives": taxes, borrowing from private credit markets, or user fees and tolls. He thereby ignored the history of the BOC from 1938 to 1974 (even though his father was once BOC Governor), but he wrote obliquely: "A government that borrows from others acquires a liability, but a government that borrows from itself may be accounted a calamity."[1] We know, of course, that no such calamity occurred over those several decades in Canada, but Coyne seems to prefer, as an ideological choice, outright privatization of all state assets.

Disrupting the Status Quo

By 2015, the CPPIB's Heather Munroe-Blum had also become a member of the (less exclusive) Trilateral Commission, where in 2015 she was joined by McKinsey's Dominic Barton and new Canadian Trilateral members like Jean Charest – the former premier of Quebec who was a key instigator of CETA and who had been booted out of office in 2012 in the wake of massive protests against his neoliberal agenda.

It looks like the "asset recycling" team was primed and ready, no matter who won the October 2015 election.

On June 8, 2016 at *The Economist's* Canada Summit conference in Toronto (yes, another one) – entitled "Disrupting the Status Quo" – PM Trudeau announced, "There is a lot of opportunity for global capital" to invest in infrastructure projects alongside Canadian pension funds.[2] Finance Minister Bill Morneau told the blue-chip crowd, "We've got these very successful investors in Canada that invest in infrastructure around the world and yet have not found the projects in Canada of the scale that makes sense for them," he said. "We'll need to ensure that there are appropriate risks and rewards for those investors."[3]

Just hours after these remarks, Morneau flew off to Dresden to attend Bilderberg 2016 from June 9 to 12.

It does make you wonder: Just who is the boss these days?

Fun Facts

One of my favourite stories about Bilderberg came out during their annual meeting in 2012, when the oligarchs met in Chantilly, Virginia. This was the infamous meeting that involved not only Alison Redford (premier of Alberta at the time), but also Nigel Wright (then chief of staff in Stephen Harper's powerful Prime Minister's Office - PMO). The day after the secret conclave ended, *The Guardian* reported that according to hotel staff, the Bilderberg attendees "don't tip," and "this year no one got anything." As writer Charlie Skelton noted, "Fair enough, there's a recession on."[4]

There's also the fun fact that the Bilderberg Steering Committee – which chooses the guests to invite and the location of each year's meeting – has an "Advisory Group" comprised of one person: David Rockefeller. I assume that makes Advisory Group meetings quite brief (though I could be wrong).

It has long been asserted – by the mainstream press and the Bilderberg attendees themselves – that Bilderberg is little more than a debating club, with the (130 or so) participants able to speak freely, knowing that what happens at Bilderberg stays at Bilderberg. But activists and writers like Daniel Estulen have debunked that notion, sharing quotes and agenda leaked by participants that reveal an elite planning process behind subsequent world events.

In a memorable comment, *The Guardian's* Charlie Skelton wrote that the Occupy movement had "demanded an end to 'our democracy representing corporations instead of the people.' What Bilderberg represents is the fact that our democracy IS our corporations. And politics is just the wake behind the shark fin."[5]

"Reasonable Returns"

On May 17, 2016 the *Globe and Mail* published an op-ed by Jean Charest, who was identified as "a partner at McCarthy Tetrault and a former premier of Quebec." Charest called the "development and redevelopment of the world's infrastructure" an "extraordinary opportunity" that could align public and private interests "with an expectation of reasonable, predictable returns over the long term."[6] Perhaps not surprisingly, Charest cited statistics from McKinsey & Co. twice in the piece.

He referred favourably to the "most recent innovation in investment models" developed by the Caisse de depot et placement du Quebec: "Under the leadership of Michael Sabia, the Caisse will finance a public transit project in Montreal valued at more than $5 billion (Canadian), featuring a new investment model. 'The government defines the public policy initiative, such as for some type of public transport infrastructure,' Mr. Sabia was quoted as saying. 'Then we take over and plan the project and do the execution. We finance the project with partners, we own it and we operate it going forward'."[7]

Charest explained, "There are two benefits generated by this type of approach, according to Mr. Sabia. First, financing costs go on the pension funds' balance sheet, not the government's. The second advantage is political. 'The person getting on a tram or crossing a bridge and paying a toll is now paying a contribution toward their pension when they do that,' [Sabia] said."[8]

Well, it's a clever argument. But the key phrase in Sabia's quoted remarks is this one: "We [the Caisse] finance the project with partners, we own it and we operate it going forward." The question is: just how long would the Caisse own and operate this project before it sells its stake to the private sector?

After Warren Buffett's Berkshire Hathaway Energy announced its $3.2 billion deal to buy Alberta's AltaLink transmission infrastructure in May 2014, I contacted B.C. financial analyst Erik Andersen, who told me that while the deal was a shock to Albertans – who had invested $16 billion into the transmission system – Buffett's takeover bid for AltaLink was "not a surprise" to the financial industry. Anderson also told me that "all P3 and IPP contracts are transferable" and "ownership moves up the food chain."[9]

So apparently there is nothing in the Caisse's "new investment model" to prevent public pension investors from later selling their stake in a P3 to private partners. Even if it's a so-called "public-public partnership," it's still a P3 and contracts are transferable to the private sector, moving ownership up the food chain.

The 24-station, automated light-rail system would connect downtown Montreal to the Trudeau airport, with the Caisse investing $3 billion and the federal and provincial governments potentitally providing the remaining $2.5 billion. Reuters has reported that the Caisse "is expecting annual returns of 10 to 15 per cent" from the project, raising concerns about the high cost of transit fares, as well as financial risk to the public as a potential "money pit".[10]

The Caisse and seven other large Canadian infrastructure investors are members of a high-powered lobby group called the Global Infrastructure Investor Association (GIIA), which includes Morgan Stanley and Goldman Sachs, and which promises on its website to ensure that any "governmental actions" that "dis-incentivise future investment are effectively addressed."

Up the Food Chain

You can't get much higher up the food chain than Bilderberg, so in April 2014 when the Ontario Liberal government of Premier Kathleen Wynne appointed Bilderberg Steering Committee member Ed Clark to lead a five-member council considering options to "optimize the full value" of provincial assets, many Ontarians were worried.

Ed Clark (President/CEO of TD Bank Group until recently) has attended 7 of the past 11 Bilderberg meetings (2006 to 2016), so you could say he's been a Bilderberg regular, along with Canadians Heather Reisman (10 out of 11), Frank McKenna (8 out of 11), and J. Robert S. Pritchard (6 out of 11). Asking a Bilderberger to choose and plan the sale of provincial assets is either extremely ignorant, or horribly naive, or blatantly compromised (or all three, if that's possible).

Back in 2009, the Liberal Dalton McGuinty government paid $200,000 to Goldman Sachs and CIBC World Markets to assess the value of provincial Crown assets, including Hydro One's 150,000 kilometres of transmission and distribution lines – one of the largest electricity transmission systems in North America. Ed Clark's council was proceeding on the basis of financial assessments already done by Goldman Sachs and CIBC. For years, the Chair of Goldman Sachs International, Peter Sutherland, has been the European Honorary Chairman of the Trilateral Commission and a regularly attending member of Bilderberg.

Ed Clark's council recommended various privatization measures, including the sell-off of Hydro One, and in June 2015 Clark was appointed as the business advisor to Premier Kathleen Wynne. At the same time, Ed Clark's son, Bert Clark, just happens to be the CEO of Infrastructure Ontario (the privatized P3 arm) in charge of the Hydro One sale – another fun fact that falls into the "everything-is-rigged" category.[11]

The Big Sell-Off

The first IPO shares sell-off of Hydro One in November 2015 was handled by a banking syndicate that included RBC Capital Markets, ScotiaBank, CIBC, TD Bank, Goldman Sachs, Barclays, Raymond James Financial, Canaccord Genuity, and Credit Suisse Securities, who made more than $29 million handling the sale.[12]

A second offering of 72.4 million Hydro One shares was conducted in April 2016 and handled by the same bankers, upping their take to nearly $60 million for the partial privatization. According to the *Globe and Mail*, "ScotiaBank spokesman Rick Roth said the process for choosing the banks to run the Hydro One IPO was handled by an 'independent committee' led by Ed Clark, the former Toronto-Dominion CEO who is now an adviser to Ms. Wynne."[13]

As of August 2016, the province of Ontario continues to hold about 71.9 per cent of Hydro One, but two more similar-sized share offerings are expected later, in a bid to raise a total of $9 billion through this "asset recycling" exercise – which is hugely unpopular. Hydro One made a profit for the province of $749 million in 2014, so it makes no sense to sell off 60 per cent to the private sector. Both opposition parties are strongly against this partial privatization.

Combined with the "cash-for-access" scandal enveloping the Ontario Liberals, the Hydro One sell-off could very well bring down the Wynne government in the coming election. Since Kathleen Wynne's swearing-in as of February 2013, the Liberal Party has held more than 150 "cash-for-access" fundraisers, including an event with executives of the banks involved in the Hydro One IPO.

On March 30, 2016, the *Globe and Mail* revealed that the Bank of Nova Scotia actively promoted a Dec. 7, 2015 Liberal fundraiser – costing $7,400 per person – featuring Finance Minister Charles Sousa and Energy Minister Bob Chiarelli. Apparently, the bank helped secure the participation of other banks involved in the Hydro One IPO. The revelation prompted CUPE President Fred Hahn to state: "These banks are using the Liberal thirst for power to drive a massive privatization agenda. It's causing history's biggest transfer of wealth from the public to the hands of a very wealthy few."[14] In mid-September, 2016 CUPE announced that it is suing the Ontario government to stop the sale of any more Hydro One shares.[15]

Privatization Agenda

In February 2014, I noticed an article in *Businessweek.com* with the following headline: "In Denmark, Goldman Sachs Deal Ignites Political Crisis." I was curious to read the piece for two initial reasons. First, I knew that Bilderberg was scheduled to meet in Denmark in May 2014 (just a few months away), and second, I knew that Goldman Sachs International Chair, Peter Sutherland, is a long-time member of Bilderberg. So the timing of Denmark's "political crisis" seemed odd; or was it the timing of the Bilderberg meeting in Denmark that was odd?

On January 29, 2014, thousands of Danish protestors gathered in front of Parliament in Copenhagen to protest the partial privatization of their nation's largest electric utility, Dong Energy. A deal had been made by the ruling Social Democrats to sell 18% of Dong Energy to Goldman Sachs for a miniscule $1.5 billion. The protestors displayed a huge banner with a drawing of a vampire squid – Matt Taibbi's memorable 2009 description of Goldman Sachs in *Rolling Stone*.

Danish fury about the sale had been growing ever since Finance Minister Bjarne Corydon announced the sale as part of a restructuring of Dong in 2013, with the $1.5 billion from Goldman Sachs to be used for building wind farms. So the Danes were being pushed into "asset recycling," like Australia. Denmark's two largest pension funds, ATP and PFA were also buying stakes in Dong at 4.9 per cent and 1.8 per cent respectively.[16]

An earlier attempt to privatize Dong Energy was made in 2004 by a former Danish government headed by Anders Fogh Rasmussen (who went on to become Secretary General of NATO from 2009 to 2014). In 2014 Rasmussen was "hired by Goldman Sachs as a political advisor in order to secure a better image of the bank among Danes."[17]

Danish Prime Minister Helle Thorning-Schmidt had won her post in 2011 through a coalition with other left-wing political parties, but after controversial austerity-style decisions - raising the pension age, cutting corporate taxes, lowering benefits to the poorest – her approval ratings had plummeted. When she then supported the Dong sale to Goldman Sachs, the Socialist People's Party pulled out of her cabinet, calling it "the last straw."[18]

By February 2014, pundits were calling the situation in Denmark a "political crisis" with the government "on the brink of collapse." Meanwhile, Bilderberg members were looking forward to their annual meeting – in May, and in Denmark.

Was the place and timing purely coincidental? It's hard to know, but what is known is that a Dong Energy executive and two Danish politicians had attended Bilderberg meetings as guests over several years, right up to 2013 when Dong was partially privatized.

Anders Eldrup, President of Dong Energy, was at Bilderberg in 2007, in 2010 (along with Poul Nyrup Rasmussen, former Danish Prime Minister), again in 2011; and in 2013 (along with Bjarne Corydon, Minister of Finance, and Michael Evans, Vice Chair of Goldman Sachs). Of course, Goldman Sach's Peter Sutherland was also at all those meetings. (And so was Ed Clark. Was he diligently taking notes and watching to see how the privatization would unfold?)

Despite opposition, the partial privatization was approved by a parliamentary committee on January 30, 2014. Poul Nyrup Rasmussen later strongly criticized the Goldman Sachs deal, calling it "a giant, historical mistake. If the Danish government must make a deal with a group of lawyers from Goldman Sachs, you have to come completely and extremely well prepared. These people are used to eating small countries for breakfast."[19]

After the Shark Fin

In June 2016, *occupy.com* updated the Dong saga, reporting: "Goldman Sachs stands to make a huge profit from the purchase of 19% of Denmark's national energy company, Dong energy, for 8 billion Danish kroner ($1.2 billion) two years ago. When Goldman bought it, the energy company was valued at $6.7 billion, a suspiciously low price ... Now, two years after the muddy affair, the energy company has been announced on the stock market and suddenly Dong Energy is valued at $15 billion. What does this mean? It means Goldman just profited by $1.7 billion in two years, since the bank's shares are now worth roughly $2.9 billion."[20]

Goldman Sachs "also gained lucrative conditions such as a veto power on the board, despite its minority share. Although the Danish state remains the majority owner of 58%, it does not have executive control over the company any more. And the deal ensured that the Danish state would cover almost any losses in the future, while Goldman would – and already did – fully benefit when Dong Energy was announced on the stock exchange."[21]

Writer Jonas Schmidt Hansen further informed readers that Danish Finance Minister Bjarne Corydon was "later rewarded for his Santa Claus role. As minister, he repeatedly spent large sums of taxpayer money for services with the powerful U.S.-based McKinsey & Company, among other consulting giants. Corydon is now positioned within a top job for McKinsey, where he is consulting private clients on opportunities for profit within the public sector, as well as advising how public sectors worldwide should run public institutions more like corporations."[22] When Corydon attended Bilderberg in 2013, he likely met and mingled with McKinsey's Ian Davis (Senior Partner Emeritus), who was there along with Dong's Anders Eldrup and Goldman Sach's two executives.

Occupy.com informs us that Goldman Sach's ownership of Dong Energy has "been placed in tax havens, so rather than contributing to the Danish welfare state, the revenues from the sale are now placed in the pockets of rich bankers offshore."[23] Bilderberg, of course, would have it no other way.

Helle Thorning-Schmidt got the brunt of the Danish people's anger, subsequently losing the election in 2015 and leaving politics in April 2016.

Usually we don't see the shark fin, only the wreckage in its wake.

15. Are Pipeline P3s in the Agenda?

Hillary Clinton wasn't the only leader who drank the McKinsey Kool-Aid by way of BlackRock's Larry Fink. Fink had been preaching against "short-termism" and "quarterly capitalism" since 2013, and in 2016 he sent a letter about it to every Fortune 500 CEO. One of the recipients was so enthused about the letter that he just had to share it with the Canadian Club in Toronto.

In his February 12, 2016 speech to the elite gathering, Brian Porter – President and CEO of Scotiabank – told them: "Early last week, Larry Fink, CEO of BlackRock – the largest global investment manager – wrote a letter to CEOs of the world's leading companies. His message was direct and simple: Instead of focusing on quarterly results, companies and investors should focus on the longer term. I liked the letter so much, I shared it with our Board of Directors and the entire senior management team at Scotiabank. ... Long-term thinking is important for all companies. And, I would also argue that it's important for all levels of government...especially during times of economic volatility."[1]

Praising the Trudeau Liberals for their support of the TransPacific Partnership, Brian Porter then turned to praising the government's "commitment to make sizeable investments in infrastructure." But he cautioned: "[C]areful thought should be given to selecting which infrastructure projects merit an investment. The government should prioritize projects that will safely move people, ideas and our abundant natural resources – projects that are environmentally and socially responsible. Projects that will create jobs and serve Canadian families and communities for years to come. One such project is the Energy East pipeline: An entirely Canadian project that is good for all Canadians ... and would create tens of thousands of jobs. It would generate billions in tax revenues and inject tens of billions into the Canadian economy. And it would also help to address Canada's startling lack of energy infrastructure in an environmentally responsible way."[2]

Calling TransCanada Corporation's Energy East pipeline "an entirely Canadian project" is certainly a clever way to spin it. The $16 billion pipeline is intended to transport tar sands diluted bitumen (dilbit) from Alberta to New Brunswick, where it would be exported to refineries mainly in the U.S. and potentially in Europe. More than 70 per cent of tar sands companies are foreign-owned, as are all the off-shore refineries.

As for those "tens of thousands of jobs," according to the Council of Canadians, the vast majority of jobs promised "would be short-term, in construction and secondary industries," while a pipeline spill from Energy East would be a major "job killer." The pipeline (actually comprised of multiple pipes) "crosses more than 900 waterways, used for drinking water, fishing, recreation and sustaining farmland."[3]

Scotiabank's Brian Porter made his remarks weeks ahead of the Liberal government's first budget in March 2016. His call for federal infrastructure funding of Energy East implies that pipelines could become P3s, whether through direct federal funding or through Canada's public pension funds.

After the *National Observer's* Mike De Souza revealed in July 2016 that two panel members of the National Energy Board (NEB) had met privately with Jean Charest while he was a paid lobbyist for TransCanada Corp., the NEB hearings on Energy East (as of early September 2016) were put on hold.

Tar Sands Investments

In 2013, Amy MacPherson revealed the extent to which the Canadian Pension Plan Investment Board (CPPIB) has been putting money into tar sands companies.[4] You can see for yourself by visiting the *CPPIB.com* website, which shows both foreign and domestic equity holdings as of March 31, 2016.

Canadians might be surprised to learn that CPPIB has invested C$286 million in TransCanada Corp. and C$357 million in Enbridge, so both companies are being supported by every Canadians' pension contributions. Other (domestic) oil sector recipients of CPPIB investment include Canadian Natural Resources Ltd. (C$294 million), Cenovus (C$86 million), Encana (C$41 million), Suncor (C$268 million) and ExxonMobil subsidiary Imperial Oil (C$34 million). More than a dozen foreign oil companies also receive CPPIB investments amounting to about C$700 million; for example: Chevron (C$111 million), ExxonMobil (C$103 million), Total (C$163 million), Royal Dutch Shell (C$30 million).

A recent article in the *National Observer* explored the CPPIB's "love affair with big oil," noting that before he left to join BlackRock, the CPPIB's Mark Wiseman had been "bullish on the fossil fuel sector" for years.[5]

The CPPIB has also invested C$1.04 billion in the Royal Bank of Canada, which happens to be the biggest financier of tar sands development.[6]

In July, an unidentified senior executive at one of Canada's biggest public pension funds told Reuters that they are now prepared to invest in new ("greenfield") infrastructure.[7]

So, supporters of Energy East or other pipelines might argue that federal infrastructure and/or P3 funding would help with a return on investment to CPPIB.

Wouldn't you know it: there's a think tank (Sustainable Prosperity) ready to promote that idea, and it even has a baby think tank offspring (Smart Prosperity) that includes Dominic Barton, Canada's "New Economy Czar."

Smart Prosperity

To be fair, the creators of Smart Prosperity don't call it "a baby think tank offspring," but rather "a new initiative launched by respected leaders to harness new thinking for Canada's environment and the economy." Their February 2016 report, called (of course) "New Thinking: Canada's Roadmap to Smart Prosperity," aims to "set Canada on the right path" through "innovative public-private partnerships" that will help us realize "the value of our marketable natural resource assets" estimated at "$750 billion."[8]

If you're thinking that none of that sounds particularly "new," then you're not being very "collaborative," which the report emphasizes (twice) is a Canadian personality trait: "Canadians are well educated, with abundant expertise in energy production, resource management, advanced manufacturing, and information technology. We are also collaborative by nature, at ease working across sectors and jurisdictions to develop creative solutions needed to capture both environmental and economic success."[9]

I predict Smart Prosperity will be pushing for pipeline P3s, largely because of who is making "Canada's roadmap" along with Dominic Barton.

Some of the Smart Prosperity members include: Lorraine Mitchelmore, Smart Prosperity Co-Chair, who until recently was the President and Chair of Shell Canada, and Michael Cruthers, the current President of Shell Canada. There's John Stackhouse, Senior Vice President of the Royal Bank of Canada, and Phil Fontaine, Special Advisor to the Royal Bank of Canada; there's Ken Neumann, Canadian National Director of the United Steel Workers. Predictably, there are some environmental collaborators: Ed Whittingham, Executive Director of the Pembina Institute; John Lounds, President & CEO of Nature Conservancy of Canada; and David Miller, President & CEO of WWF-Canada.[10]

No doubt, McKinsey's Dominic Barton can work with these people.

The "W" Word

In 2009 Barton was interviewed by the *Globe and Mail*, which summarized his view of Canadians as being "strangely reticent" on "issues where we should be leading," such as "the future of water. Canada has close to 6 per cent of the world's renewable water, but he fears it does not play a heavyweight role in international discussion of water's geopolitical future."[11]

In 2013, Barton gave a speech in which he said, "In 2009, McKinsey worked with the World Bank, the International Finance Corporation [IFC] and six companies that are big water users, including Coca Cola and Nestle, to estimate water supply and demand up to the year 2030. What we discovered is that if we stay on the current trajectory of usage, and even accounting for technological innovation, demand for water will exceed supply by 40% within two decades. Since water does not follow political boundaries, shortages will have far-reaching implications."[12]

A 2012 report by Corporate Accountability International revealed that the World Bank's IFC provides an informal "stamp of approval" for water privatization projects, thereby attracting funding from private and other outside sources.[14] As a result, Wall Street banksters are buying up the world's water, as writer Jo-Shing Yang has thoroughly documented: "Goldman Sachs, JP Morgan Chase, Citigroup, UBS, Deutsche Bank, Credit Suisse, Macquarie Bank, Barclays Bank, the Blackstone Group, Allianz and HSBC Bank, among others, are consolidating their control over water," often by partnering "with regional public-sector pension funds and with sovereign wealth funds."[13]

Bank of America Merrill Lynch predicts "a water market worth over $1 trillion by 2020."[15]

With a Bank of America Merrill Lynch banker advising the Trudeau government on setting up a Canadian Infrastructure Bank, and with McKinsey's Dominic Barton acting as Canada's New Economy Czar, it's logical to ask: is bulk water export being discussed behind closed doors by the federal government?

On May 20, 2016 international relations expert Parag Khanna told CBC Radio's *The Current* that the U.S. needs Canada's water. In his book *Connectography: Mapping the Future of Global Civilization*, Khanna writes that "the time has come to dust off schemes such as the renowned Canadian engineer Tom Kieran's Great Recycling and Northern Development [Grand] Canal and the ill-fated 1970s North American Water and Power

Alliance (NAWAPA)" proposed by California's Ralph Parsons Engineering. These proposals would "capture river runoff as far north as Canada's Yukon and Hudson's Bay and channel it ... into man-made reservoirs and interbasin canals" for export.[16]

Site C

In July 2016 the Trudeau government approved two permits for the controversial Site C dam in northeastern B.C., raising widespread anger because court challenges to the project are underway. This proposed 60-metre high and 1,050-metre dam on the Peace River, if built, would create an 83 kilometre reservoir submerging First Nations unceded territory and heritage sites, and permanently flooding some of the best agricultural land in the province.

Agrologist Wendy Holm and others such as Jennifer O'Keeffe have warned that Site C "falls directly on the lines drawn in the original NAWAPA plans. Site C and the Columbia River Project are integral to the implementation of NAWAPA, thus calling into question the nature of the project in relationship to continental water diversion plans."[17] O'Keeffe recently explained that, "once impounded behind the dam, the Peace River is subject to NAFTA as a water commodity, thus putting the people of Canada at risk of losing water rights if privatization of BC Hydro occurs." [18]

O'Keeffe also questioned whether BC Hydro's fiscal mismanagement and debt are "a primer for manufactured privatization to occur." Since 2001, B.C. Liberal governments have transformed the Crown corporation from a generator of publicly-owned electricity to a purchaser of independent power production (IPP).[19] The resulting fiscal mess ($55 billion debt) and rising prices are similar to what happened in Ontario, leading to the ongoing selloff of a majority stake in Hydro One. Damien Gillis wrote in 2013 that the same pattern has been repeated around the world to privatize public assets like BC Hydro and "they will try to do it here [in B.C.] next."[20]

At this point, it's worth mentioning that Shell Canada has a 5,000-cubic-metre-a-day water licence on the Peace River.[21] Shell, you'll recall, has two members on that baby think tank offspring called Smart Prosperity, along with Dominic Barton. As well, the biggest shareholder in Shell is BlackRock, and CPPIB has $30 million invested in Shell.

The Shutdown

To the shock of many, suddenly in March 2016, one of Canada's most effective water study programs closed its doors. The Program on Water Issues (POWI), directed by Adele Hurley, had for 15 years been part of the University of Toronto's Munk School of Global Affairs. POWI closed because it lost its funding from a private Toronto-based philanthropy called the Walter and Duncan Gordon Foundation.

As Andrew Nikiforuk reported, POWI conducted important research and debate on "oil sands water withdrawals from the Athabasca River, groundwater monitoring, climate change, the future of the Columbia River Treaty, and the impacts of hydraulic fracking on groundwater. The program also played a pivotal role in helping to draft federal legislation in 2013 that banned bulk water exports, as well as an international agreement that prevented the diversion of water from the Great Lakes Region."[22]

No one could or would explain to Nikiforuk why the Walter and Duncan Gordon Foundation pulled its funding from POWI. After talking with renowned water ecologist David Schindler, Nikiforuk wrote that "the program may have done its job too well and rattled corporate interests, suggested Schindler."[23]

Because Gordon Foundation Chair Robert Pace is also Chair of the Canadian National Railway (which transports frac sand and fracked oil), Nikiforuk explored the possibility that POWI funding had been withdrawn because the Program had conducted three conferences on fracking. But the Gordon Foundation told him that Robert Pace had played no role in the decision.[24]

However, for alert readers of the book in hand, it's important to raise another possibility.

The private Walter and Duncan Gordon Foundation has the motto "Protecting Canada's Water. Empowering Canada's North." Its website lists six partners in that goal: the Munk School (likely no longer a partner now); an NGO called Living Lakes Canada; an industry initiative called

Canadian Water Network (where Robert Pace is on the Board); another NGO called Canadian Freshwater Alliance; and two more partners: the Royal Bank of Canada, and the WWF.

You'll recall that the Smart Prosperity "initiative" has two members from the Royal Bank of Canada and one member from WWF, along with Shell's two members and Dominic Barton, etc. Could the Royal Bank of Canada and WWF have quietly urged their Gordon Foundation partner to pull the plug on funding for POWI? It's certainly convenient for the corporate sector to no longer have an independent outfit like POWI examining fresh water issues in Canada.

In October 2014, a Council on Foreign Relations Task Force (with members from Goldman Sachs, ExxonMobil, and other investors) issued a report calling for "the North American community" to address "the diversion of water from one watershed to another" and "regional cooperation because demands on limited water resources will grow."[25] For its part, the Obama administration has said that California's water challenges are a top priority and it has been pushing, along with state officials, to build massive water tunnels to bring water to southern regions of the drought-parched state.[26] Hillary Clinton has promised that, if elected, she will continue with such top priorities.

16. Lessons from Iceland

John Perkins' 2004 best-seller, *Confessions of An Economic Hit Man*, had revealed in devastating detail how consultants like himself had coerced Third World governments during the late 1960s and 1970s to take on huge loans from the World Bank, the IMF, and other lending agencies in order to build vast infrastructure projects.[1] The money went directly to U.S. engineering and construction firms like Bechtel, Halliburton, Stone & Webster, Brown & Root, and other contracting, consulting and engineering firms, who profited immensely from such projects. Once a country had been saddled with massive foreign debt, it could be manipulated and further coerced into working on behalf of the multinationals. It could also be financially ruined by that debt.

That's what happened to Iceland on October 6, 2008, when its banks collapsed and the country went belly-up. Perkins said there was "every indication" that Iceland had been "targeted by economic hit men [EHM]." He even publicly called Iceland "an experiment in the process of 'how do we hit developed countries'."

Perkins' popular books and speaking tours were reaching millions by the time of Iceland's banking fiasco, and when it became known that Perkins had been asked to advise the Icelandic government on how to handle the situation, consultants like McKinsey & Company must have been shuddering. That may be why almost all news about Iceland's economic turmoil was kept out of corporate media until about 2012 – preventing the public from learning an entirely different way of dealing with the banksters.

Targeted by EHM

Perkins' 2009 book *Hoodwinked* opens with his March 2009 trip to Iceland, including a memorable drive into Reykjavik, where Perkins saw rows and rows of suburban houses "all vacant," and magnificent modern office buildings "now empty." This was evidence of the sudden collapse of the banks, which punctured the housing bubble, leaving dozens of unoccupied homes and buildings.

Perkins provides some details about how Iceland got into massive debt. With its abundant hydroelectric and geothermal potential, Iceland was targeted in the 1990s by "the biggest of the energy users, the aluminum companies," which convinced Iceland's leaders "to construct power plants for the sole purpose of energizing foreign-owned smelters ... All Iceland had to do was commit to a very large loan – collateralized by the revenues anticipated from the sale of kilowatt-hours – and hire foreign corporations to build a dam and power plant to generate over 600 megawatts" to fire one aluminum smelter.[2]

The Icelandic government waived environmental laws and issued permits for Alcoa's massive project to be built by Bechtel Corporation and others – despite the grave environmental dangers predicted for eastern Iceland. (Bechtel, by the way, is the lead member of the corporate team building the controversial Keeyask hydroelectric dam in Manitoba.)[3]

Meanwhile, writes Perkins, "economic hit men arrived in droves [in Iceland]. Morgan Stanley, Goldman Sachs, and most of the other big Wall Street firms dispatched their necktied armies. Applying a model similar to that used to exploit Indonesia, Nigeria, Colombia, and all the countries whose oil or other precious natural resources propelled them into instant materialism, men and women with my old job convinced individuals and the government to mortgage to the hilt."[4] Barclays arranged the final loan required by Iceland's national electricity company to build the vast dam and power plant complex needed to run Alcoa's smelter.[5]

Boom & Bust

Between 2002 and 2007, when Alcoa inaugurated its aluminum factory, Iceland's stock market skyrocketed, bank lending ballooned into the stratosphere (with the banks themselves borrowing more than $120 billion from foreign lenders), and Reykjavik's real estate prices tripled. Perkins wrote, "The people celebrated – that is, until they learned that their utility company was hemorrhaging tens of thousands of dollars every hour that Alcoa ran its equipment."[6] The Icelandic government had contracted to provide Alcoa with such "cheap energy" that the Icelanders were not only saddled with huge debt (US$5 billion) for the dam and power plant, but were themselves subsidizing Alcoa's massive energy use by about US$200 million annually. Every megawatt for Alcoa "cost the country hundreds of thousands of dollars," Perkins has said publicly.

Such a debt-fuelled boom (backed by foreign lending) was unstable, and when Lehman Brothers collapsed in the U.S., Iceland's banks quickly followed. One financial analyst explained: "By 2008, the [Icelandic] banks' balance sheets had grown to more than 10 times [the] country's entire annual economic output, with many of the assets in foreign currencies and backed by short-term borrowing. When funding markets shut after the Lehman Brothers failure in the U.S., Iceland's top banks collapsed in quick succession, hitting depositors and creditors."[7]

Michael Lewis visited Iceland for his 2011 book, *Boomerang: Travels in the New Third World*. He wrote: "When their three brand-new global-size banks collapsed, Iceland's 300,000 citizens found that they bore some kind of responsibility for $100 billion in banking losses – which works out to roughly $330,000 for every Icelandic man, woman and child."[8] Icelanders also had billions in personal losses from currency speculation and from the collapse of the stock market.

While nothing could be done about some elements of that huge financial hole, Icelanders refused responsibility for the $100 billion in private banking losses. As economist Michael Hudson wrote in 2009:

"The European Union and International Monetary Fund have told them to replace private debts with public obligations, and to pay by raising taxes, slashing public spending and obliging citizens to deplete their savings. Resentment is growing not only toward those who ran up these debts ... but also toward the neoliberal foreign advisors and creditors..."[9]

Not Too Big To Jail

Perkins doesn't say in *Hoodwinked* what advice he gave the Icelandic government, but in a later interview he said he encouraged them "not to repay their debts,"[10] and in an Icelandic TV interview of February 2009, he said Iceland should not accept a bailout loan from the IMF, and instead "send it packing."

Iceland, however, did agree to a $4.36 billion IMF bailout of its banks, but apparently managed to negotiate the loan on its own favourable terms and to conduct a recovery in its own unique way.

As *Common Ground's* Geoff Olson wrote, "the Icelanders were in no mood to take a post-meltdown economic prescription from the sources that had sickened them in the first place. Icelanders nationalized one bank, put three others into receivership and instituted capital controls. Told they could no longer expect the same standard of education and health care that their parents had taken for granted, Iceland went it alone and managed their own affairs. Most notably, authorities indicted Icelandic banker Sigurdur 'Siggi' Einarsson, head of the Kaupthing bank, along with nine senior executives. Bailouts, nei. Jail-ins, ja."[11]

Icelanders took to the streets, banging pots and pans and refusing to pay for the sins of the bankers through tax measures. Instead, they insisted on the arrest and prosecution of dozens of bankers responsible for the economic collapse, forced their entire government to resign, and created a citizens' group tasked with writing a new constitution protecting the country from corporate greed – all the while actually expanding their social safety net. But as one writer noted in 2013, "the U.S. media has essentially skipped over this [Icelandic] story for the past five years."[12]

No wonder: the Icelanders were not only refusing to play along with the usual EHM script, they were putting banksters in jail and defying the gospel about bailing out private banks – instead, making the banks' shareholders take the losses. Foreign creditors howled, but Icelanders shrugged, then nationalized the failing banks, forcing them to reduce excessive mortgage debt, which saved many homeowners from foreclosure.

By October 2015, Iceland had put 26 banksters behind bars, serving terms of two to five years, for crimes including market manipulation, embezzlement, and breach of fiduciary duties. By December 2015, Iceland had also managed to pay off its IMF debt in full,[13] mainly because the country did something really smart at the outset of the crisis: it slapped on capital controls.

Capital Controls

As *The Economist* explained: "In the years before the crisis, investors had piled into Icelandic assets, and Icelanders themselves had taken out plenty of debt denominated in foreign currencies (because that foreign-denominated debt carried lower interest rates than those on offer in the Icelandic currency, the krona). When the banking crisis hit, the krona plunged in value because investors started to convert their Icelandic assets into foreign currencies. A collapsed krona would have been fatal for Iceland's economy, for two reasons. First, Icelandic households would not have been able to repay their foreign-currency debt (since their earnings were in kronur). Second, a collapsed currency would have provoked high inflation, since Iceland's substantial flow of imports would have become extremely expensive. That, in turn, would have left many Icelanders – and even those without foreign-currency debt – in real trouble, since many Icelandic loans were indexed to inflation."[14]

Capital controls are especially important in a globalized financial world where traders move money around in nanoseconds and profit on currency speculation.

The Economist noted: "Capital controls protected Iceland in a few ways. They slowed capital flight; investors that had built up big positions in Icelandic assets were prevented from selling them, converting the proceeds to foreign currency and yanking them out of the country. Hedge funds that had snapped up the assets of the failed banks could not remove their booty from the country. The controls also limited the extent to which investors holding krona-denominated assets abroad could get a hard-currency return. They prevented those assets from being brought back to Iceland and sold for kronur, which then might have been readily exchanged for other currencies. These limits kept the krona from depreciating as much as it otherwise would have done."[15]

But the reason that Iceland was able to institute such capital controls is that it is not part of the EU and it has its own currency. Those factors gave the country more latitude than Greece or other EU members dealing with financial collapse.[16] If you don't have your own currency or monetary control as a sovereign nation, there is little you can do to alter your financial situation. Not surprisingly, most Icelanders lost any desire to join the EU, although a previous government had applied to join in 2009. The current government has cancelled the application.

It's important to recall, however, that pending trade agreements like TISA would prevent the use of capital controls in the future.

Recovery

Iceland's handling of the banking debacle – especially its jailing of the banksters – is admired by many across the planet, and the country's economy is now said to be recovering well and faster than expected. But Iceland will be paying for Alcoa's "cheap energy" for five decades, and it will take many years for the public to pay off the loans that built the dam and power plants so that Alcoa and other aluminum manufacturers can pocket hundreds of millions in profits every year.

Iceland's foremost environmental organization, Saving Iceland, has been documenting the continual destruction caused by the smelters and dams: escalating greenhouse gases, fluoride pollution that is killing farm animals, dead rivers, destruction of reindeer calving grounds, drought in areas where rivers were diverted away, etc. Canadian geothermal company Alterra Power is also criticized for exploitation in the same region. Even so, by 2015 Icelandic politicians were considering building at least eight more power complexes, and calling them "clean energy."[17]

Perhaps in exasperation, in April 2016 Iceland elected a political outsider as its president. Gudni Johannesson, a professor of history and an expert on the constitution, campaigned on the promise to institute a constitutional clause allowing citizen-initiated referendums over parliamentary bills.[18]

The COMER lawsuit has apparently inspired Icelanders, who are considering taking the money-creation function away from private banks and returning it to Iceland's central bank and Parliament. The COMER newsletter commented, "Good for Iceland! An immensely important feature of their proposal is that they recognize the crucial need to keep the power to create money and the power to decide how that money is used in Parliament. Parliament [would] debate the government's proposal for the allocation of new money. What else could make sense in a truly democratic society?"[19]

Iceland has also been considering a system of public banks, modeled on Sparkassen in Germany.[20] Obviously, the banking and economic turmoil of the past eight years has pushed people into new ways of thinking. As one writer put it, "Who knew that the revolution would start with those radical Icelanders?"[21]

Michael Lewis likely suspected it after his visit there. He wrote in 2011 about his impression of Icelanders: "They have a feral streak in them, like a horse that's just pretending to be broken."[22]

Conclusion: A Dangerous Combination

At Ottawa's Westin Hotel in mid-April 2016, a handful of Canadian public officials engaged in a weird kind of speed-dating with private-sector members lusting after infrastructure P3s. The event was part of something called the P3 Hub Ottawa, offered by the Canadian Council for Public-Private Partnerships (CCPPP) with the agenda entitled "Canada: What Next? Delivering Infrastructure in the New Canada."

At the April 18th Roundtables, participants were promised: "Each of our public officials will rotate around tables of 10 and spend 20 minutes on each table answering questions and discussing P3 opportunities for the future. They will look at how their private sector partners can better assist in procurement and what kind of partnerships they are seeking."

I have no idea how much the private participants paid for those 20-minute interactions with public officials rotating around tables, but it was likely worth the money. After all, they were getting face-time with John McBride, CEO of PPP Canada; Jean-Francois Tremblay, Deputy Minister at Infrastructure Canada; Josh Colle, Chair of Toronto Transit Commission; and Medlinda Nycholat, Vice President at Defence Construction Canada.

During the main event on April 19th, officials proudly presented a "case study" of "one of Canada's largest and most complex PPPs," the new headquarters for the Communications Security Establishment (CSE) – i.e., the spooks.

Spy Palace

Rumour has it that well over $1 billion was spent on the spy palace for the CSE, which P3 Hub Ottawa described in these words: "The Communications Security Establishment Canada ('CSE') is Canada's national cryptologic agency. CSE is one of Canada's key security and intelligence organizations, focused on collecting foreign signals intelligence in support of the Government of Canada's priorities, and on helping protect the computer networks and information of greatest importance to Canada. When the Government of Canada undertook this challenging project, they turned to PPP because of the performance-based approach to building and maintaining critical infrastructure and facilities. The new headquarters has been occupied for 18 months and is supporting the CSE mission."

A CSE executive, Michael Komery, was at P3 Hub Ottawa to explain the P3 financing arrangements for the new headquarters. Komery's title is Director General of Corporate Services Operations – Communications Security Establishment Canada. Just what are "Corporate Services Operations"? I have not been able to pin that down, but they sound like every activist's worst nightmare. CSE oversees CSIS (the Canadian Security Intelligence Service), which oversees the rest of us.

It seems fitting that 2016 P3 Hub Ottawa would tout the spy palace as its shining example of the P3 process in action. This, after all, is a government that backed the draconian anti-terrorism Bill C-51 (passed in June 2015), while promising to amend it if elected. As we approach the first anniversary of the Trudeau Liberals in power, questions have been raised about just how willing they are to scrap or restrict C-51.

The Liberals are moving to create an all-party national security oversight committee, described as "toothless" by *Rabble.ca*'s J. Baglow because the "oversight" only kicks in "long after the bad decisions have already been made by low-level operatives."[1] Similarly, David Christopher wrote that "… the spy agencies are already exploiting the sweeping new powers bestowed upon them by Bill C-51. As Jim Bronskill of the Canadian Press wrote earlier this year, at least four federal agencies, including CSIS, are already using the legislation to gain access to Canadians' private information. And CSIS head Michel Coulombe recently told parliamentarians that his agency has already used C-51s extraordinary 'disruption' powers over two dozen times without seeking judicial approval."[2]

In March 2016, Coulombe also warned parliamentarians that any attempt to downplay or discount terrorists' threats to Canada could lead to a potential "lack of confidence among our partners in the United States."[3] That may be the real reason for not repealing the legislation, although *Globe and Mail* columnist Lawrence Martin noted in August that the Liberals "now feel a new need to be cautious. What if, an insider explained, the Liberals brought in big-time amendments to defang C-51 and there was a subsequent terrorist act on Canadian soil: 'How would we look then?'"[4]

New Gestapo

Not everyone is so willing to sacrifice their civil liberties. Many Canadian legal experts have voiced their opposition to C-51 and continue to do so.

At an anti-C-51 Toronto rally in May 2015 (before the bill was passed), constitutional lawyer Rocco Galati told the crowd, "What this legislation creates, and make no mistake about it, is a modern day Gestapo, no exaggeration. It chills, censors, and criminalizes free speech, free association, and constitutional rights of assembly. This legislation is not new. German and Italian versions were passed in the 1930s in Europe and they looked very much like C-51."[5]

As reported by *Press For Truth*, Galati outlined five dangers in the legislation:

1) It takes the private information of Canadian citizens and shares it with all government agencies, including foreign governments. "For some Canadian citizens," Galati told the crowd, "that becomes an eventuality of torture and or death when they are traveling abroad."

2) It arbitrarily restricts who can travel.

3) It makes political criticism a terrorist offense in itself. "So words

and thoughts become an act of terrorism under this bill," Galati explained.

4) It allows CSIS to covertly disrupt constitutionally-protected rights of association, expression and protest.

5) It does all this by removing transparent judicial oversight.[6]

Like many others, Galati has given a clear warning about the direction that such legislation is pushing Canada.

As we know from the experience of Occupy Wall Street, U.S. Homeland Security and the NYPD teamed up with Wall Street banks to shut down protests; infiltrate, spy on and arrest activists; and even considered them to be "terrorists." This was an astonishing criminalization of activists working peacefully to protest the rising financial oligarchy.

Beyond the Border

But it isn't just C-51 that is problematic for civil liberties and democratic rights in Canada. Bill C-13, Bill C-44, and Bill C-639 (also passed during the Harper reign) similarly expand surveillance and restrict citizens' rights of assembly in order to protect "critical infrastructure."[7] In particular, C-639 dovetails with the Canada-U.S. Beyond the Border Action Plan, which is the result of perimeter security and economic integration talks secretly launched by the U.S. and Canada in 2010.

The protection of shared critical infrastructure is listed as a priority in security documents on the government's Beyond the Border website. The documents state: "Canada and the United States share a significant quantity of critical infrastructure assets and systems, including pipelines, the electric grid, and transportation systems. It is imperative that our countries work together to protect these assets. To effectively do this, our governments will require a close collaboration with the private sector, as they own much critical infrastructure in question."[8]

C-639 criminalizes peaceful protests if they interfere even temporarily with broadly defined "critical infrastructure," imposing a mandatory minimum sentence of two to 10 years imprisonment and fines up to $3,000. "Critical infrastructure" is so broadly defined in C-639 that it could be anything: "services relating to energy, telecommunications, finance, health care, food, water transportation, public safety, government and manufacturing, the disruption of which could produce serious adverse economic effects or endanger the health or safety of Canadians."

The B.C. Civil Liberties Association considers C-639 a direct attack on the Canadian Constitution and Charter rights, and has said the legislation shows the Canadian government is "borrowing tactics from dictatorial governments."[9]

Dangerous Combination

Draconian legislation is not the only challenge facing us. Combined with trade deals that greatly prohibit any attempts to curtail the corporate sector (especially the financial sector), we are being herded in an extreme direction: not only to give up our civil liberties, but to accept corporate rule - even as we are told to sell off our public infrastructure because of (neoliberalism imposed) government debt.

COMER's Ann Emmett told me bluntly that we are moving toward a dangerous combination of "fascism and feudalism" that must be stopped.

Chris Hedges wrote in his 2015 book called *Wages of Rebellion*: "I do not know if we can build a better society. I do not even know if we will survive as a species. But I do know that these corporate forces have us by the throat. And they have my children by the throat. I do not fight fascists because I will win. I fight fascists because they are fascists."[10]

In January 2016, Oxfam released a report showing that 62 billionaires own as much wealth as half the world's population. Between 2010 and 2015, the wealth of the poorest dropped by 41% – a gushing of money and assets ($500 billion) to the oligarchy just in those five years.[11]

Now that we are in the vice-grip of financial instability, our elected leaders admonish us to continually cave to the corporate sector, even when their infrastructure projects will benefit only a tiny elite, while ruining the world of the rest. B.C. premier Christy Clark recently said, "I'm always of the view that you should try and find a way to get to yes on economic projects. We need resource extraction in Canada if we want to have all the things that matter to us, like health care and education and low taxes. So we've set out the path to yes for Kinder Morgan" and its pipeline expansion project.[12]

There's that "strange blackout of national memory" again. But as COMER reminds us, we had "health care and education and low taxes" for 35 years by borrowing from the Bank of Canada. We don't need to be herded into "resource extraction" that basically only benefits the bottom-line of a few (mostly foreign) corporations. Indeed, according to the leading authority on tar sands royalty rates, Barry Rodgers, as of January 2016 Alberta had "the lowest royalty rates in the world," and that was before the NDP government reduced them even further in July.[13] It's likely the oil billionaires find this hilarious as they advocate for pipelines to reach tidewater.

In 2007, author John Perkins noted that the oligarchy seems "determined to return to the monopolistic trusts of the late 1800s," but this time "happening on a global scale."[14] After his 2009 trip to Iceland, Perkins warned that the economic hit men had now targeted the U.S. He'd likely say the same thing about Canada. Michael Lewis' 2011 book also hinted at what's happening: the developed world is fast becoming "the New Third World" – a kind of financial karmic boomerang that bodes ill for anyone who cares about democracy, civil rights, the environment, and social justice.

As the COMER folks, the proponents of public banking, and others keep reminding us, it doesn't have to be this way.

Acknowledgements

Thanks to Ann Emmett, who gave me books and materials from her library and answered many questions. Herb Wiseman was also helpful in providing information and explanations. Of course, any mistakes or errors are mine. The Writers Trust, Ed Finn and my brother Chuck Nelson provided some financial support for the months of research and writing. I also want to thank the many writers and publications that I have quoted and footnoted. Portions of this book originally appeared in *Economic Reform*, *Watershed Sentinel* and *counterpunch.org*. As usual, I am grateful to G.S. and G.G. for their help.

Thanks also to the volunteer proofreaders from *Watershed Sentinel* who helped spot glitches.

Endnotes

Introduction
[1] David Macdonald, "Canada's Banks Lavished with $108 Billion in Government Aid," *CCPA Monitor*, May 2012.
[2] Ibid.
[3] Peter Henderson, "Did Canadian Banks Receive a Secret Bailout?" *Financial Post*, April 30, 2012.
[4] Quoted in Ed Finn, "What We Need to Know about Neoliberalism (Before It's Too Late)," *rabble.ca*, May 12, 2016.
[5] David Rosen, "Are We Entering an Era of Postmodern Serfdom?" *counterpunch.org*, July 8, 2016.
[6] Linda McQuaig, "Plutocracy Awaits Us," in Ed Finn, Editor, *Canada After Harper: His Ideology-Fuelled Attack on Canadian Society and Values, and How We Can Resist and Create the Country We Want*, Toronto: James Lorimer & Company Ltd., 2015, pp. 153-158.
[7] Andrew Gavin Marshall, "No Conspiracy Theory – A Small Group of Companies Have Enormous Power Over the World," *alterNet.org*, October 31, 2012.
[8] Ellen Brown, "Brexit and the Derivatives Time Bomb," Web of Debt blog, (*ellenbrown.com*), July 2, 2016.
[9] Judy Kennedy, "Money Matters – COMER v. Canada," *Economic Reform*, July-August, 2015.
[10] George Monbiot, "Break the grip of corporate power to secure our future," *The Guardian*, December 3, 2012.
[11] Brown, op. cit.
[12] Matt Taibbi, "The Vampire Squid Strikes Again: The Mega Banks' Most Devious Scam Yet," *Rolling Stone*, February 12, 2014.
[13] Peter Phillips and Brady Osborne, "Exposing the Financial Core of the Transnational Capitalist Class," *globalresearch.ca*, September 13, 2013.
[14] Herb Wiseman, "Capitulating to Capitalism: The Market Place as a Bully," *Economic Reform*, February 2006.
[15] Ed Finn, "Most people know less about money than nuclear fission," *CCPA Monitor*, July/August, 1997.
[16] Murray Dobbin, "Liberate the Bank of Canada, Intrepid Think Tank Urges," *thetyee.ca*, April 17, 2015.

1. Bank of Canada Lawsuit
[1] Les Whittington, "Rocco Galati in Court to Challenge How Bank of Canada Does Business," *Toronto Star*, March 23, 2015.
[2] Bill Abram, *Canadian Monetary History*, Maple Bay: C&W Publishing, 2008.
[3] Murray Dobbin, "Opinion: Liberate the Bank of Canada, Intrepid Think Tank Urges," *thetyee.ca*, April 17, 2015.
[4] "Manufacturing Consent or Why Our Eyes Are Wide Shut," *Economic Reform*, September-October, 2015.
[5] Liberal Party Backgrounder, "An Historic Investment Plan to Strengthen the Middle Class, Create Jobs, and Grow Our Economy," August, 2015.
[6] Ibid.
[7] Paul Krugman, "Keynes Comes to Canada," *New York Times*, October 23, 2015.

2. The Rise of the Overlords
[1] Quoted in Bill Abram, *Canadian Monetary History*, Maple Bay, B.C.: C&W Publishing, 2008, p. 16.
[2] Quoted in William F. Hixson, *It's Your Money*, London, Ont.: COMER Publications, 1997, p. 1.
[3] Abram, op. cit., p. 23.
[4] Paul T. Hellyer, *The Money Mafia: A World In Crisis*, Walterville, Oregon: Trine Day LLC, 2014, p. 97.
[5] Peter Dolack, "Today's Economic Hard Times Are the Culmination of a Long Series of Crises," *truthout.org*, August 23, 2016.
[6] Naomi Klein, *The Shock Doctrine: The Rise of Disaster Capitalism*, Toronto: Vintage Canada, 2008.

[7] Quoted in ibid., p.112.

[8] Michel Chossudovsky, "Understand the Globalization of Poverty and the New World Order," *globalresearch.ca*, August 9, 2016.

[9] Ibid.

[10] Murray Dobbin, "Liberate the Bank of Canada, Intrepid Think Tank Urges," *thetyee.ca*, April 17, 2015.

[11] Abram, op. cit., p. 11.

[12] Charles Higham, *Trading with the Enemy: An Exposé of The Nazi-American Money Plot, 1933-1949*, New York: Delacorte Press, 1983.

[13] Adam Lebor, *Tower of Basel: The Shadowy History of the Secret Bank That Runs the World*, New York: Perseus Books Group, 2013, p. 176.

[14] Ibid., p. xxi

[15] Quoted in Ellen Brown, "Canada's 2012 Budget: Imposing Austerity on the World's Most Resource-Rich Country," *commondreams.ca*, April 1, 2012.

[16] Jim Mars, *The Trillion-Dollar Conspiracy*, New York, London, Toronto, Sydney: Harper Collins, 2010, p. 72.

[17] Hellyer, op. cit., p. 62.

[18] John Perkins, *Confessions of an Economic Hit Man*, New York: Penguin Books, 2004.

[19] Donald Gutstein, *Harperism: How Stephen Harper and his Think Tank Colleagues Have Transformed Canada*, Toronto: James Lorimer & Company Ltd., 2014, p.12.

[20] Greg Palast, *Vulture's Picnic*, New York: Penguin Group, 2011, p. 275.

[21] William Krehm, *A Power Unto Itself: The Bank of Canada*, Toronto: Stoddart, 1993, pp. 29-30.

[22] Andy Blatchford, "Will Big Pension Funds and Ottawa Partner to Build Tomorrrow's Infrastructure?" Canadian Press, May 15, 2016.

[23] Quoted in Abram, op. cit., p. 13.

[24] Klein, op. cit., p.66.

3. A 21ˢᵗ Century Trojan Horse

[1] "COMER Case Against Bank of Canada Reaches Its End," *pressfortruth.ca*, February 25, 2016.

[2] Rocco Galati, "Decision of Federal Court, February 8, 2016," *Economic Reform*, January-February, 2016.

[3] Gordon Isfeld, "Stephen Poloz Defends the Central Bank's Independence from Finance Department," *Financial Post*, April 13, 2016.

[4] Sheldon Gordon, "Building Infrastructure: The Legal Framework for Canada's Push," *Lexpert Magazine*, April, 2016.

[5] Jason Fekete, "Stakes are Huge as Liberal Government Moves Forward on Canada Infrastructure Bank," *Ottawa Citizen*, March 18, 2016.

[6] Pam Martens and Russ Martens, "One Forgotten Document Casts Embarrassing Light on Krugman's 'Sanders Over the Edge' Column," *wallstreetonparade.com*, April 12, 2016.

[7] Matt Taibbi, "Bank of America: Too Crooked to Jail," *Rolling Stone*, March 29, 2012.

[8] "The Rise of BlackRock," *The Economist*, December 7, 2013.

[9] Ibid.

[10] "The Monolith and the Markets," *The Economist*, December 7, 2013.

[11] Katrina Brooker, "Can This Man Save Wall Street?" *Fortune*, November 10, 2008.

[12] *Business Wire*, "BlackRock Announces Appointment of Gordon M. Nixon to Board of Directors," July 30, 2015.

[13] "The Monolith and the Markets," op. cit.

[14] Ibid.

[15] Ryan Tracy and Sarah Krouse, "One Firm Getting What It Wants in Washington: BlackRock," *The Wall Street Journal*, April 20, 2016.

[16] Ibid.

[17] Ellen Brown, "Our Banks Own Airports, Control Power Plants and Much More - How Can We Stop Them from Controlling the Lifelines of the Economy?" *alternet.org*, August 26, 2013.

[18] Adam Mayers, "Why the CPP is Snapping Up Ports and Dorms: Mayers," *Toronto Star*, March 7, 2016.

[19] Scott Deveau (Bloomberg), "Canadian Pension Funds Urge Trudeau to Think Big on Infrastructure: 'We're Looking for Projects of Scale'," *Financial Post*, March 16, 2016.

[20] Ibid.

[21] Daniel Hurst and Paul Farrell, "Senate Blocks Government's 'Asset Recycling' Model," *The Guardian*, July 18, 2014.

[22] CUPE, "Ours to Keep: Municipal Public Services and Assets," *cupe.ca*, May 28, 2015.

[23] *Canadian Press*, "Hydro One Debuts On TSX In Canada's Largest IPO In 15 Years," November 5, 2015.

[24] Benjamin Dachis, "Getting More Buildings for our Bucks: Canadian Infrastructure Policy in 2016," The C.D. Howe Institute, January 13, 2016.

[25] Joyce Nelson, "The Rockefeller Files, Part 3: Ontario Election and Privatization," *Rabble.ca*, June 6, 2014.

[26] Andy Blatchford (Canadian Press), "Liberals Consider Non-government Investors to Help Pay for Infrastructure," *Toronto Star*, April 24, 2015.

[27] Ibid.

[28] Amy MacPherson, "Where Your CPP Money Really Goes: Parts 1 & 2," *Huffington Post*, January 17 and 22, 2013.

[29] Mark Wiseman, "Building the Case for a Long-Term Perspective," CPP Investment Board, September 16, 2015.

[30] Kevin Skerrett, "Pension Funds Investing in Privatization of Infrastructure," *cupe.ca*, June 28, 2016.

[31] Reuters, "Canada's Pension Funds Showing Growing Dominance," *Financial Post*, January 12, 2012.

[32] The Canadian Press, "TransCanada Cuts Ties with U.S. Public Relations Firm Edelman," *CBC News*, November 26, 2014.

[33] Rafe Mair, "A PR Flack's Guide to LNG: Dream Team tries to repair industry's image," *commonsensecanadian.ca*, March 15, 2015.

[34] Gary Mason, "Alberta, B.C. Discuss Deal to Swap Pipeline for Electricity," *The Globe & Mail*, April 20, 2016.

[35] "The Rise of BlackRock," op. cit.

[36] Maude Barlow and Paul Moist, "With Trade Deal, Will Canada Give EU 'Right to Profit' on Water?" *thetyee.ca*, February 2, 2012.

[37] CUPE, "Ours to Keep," op. cit.

[38] Rob Ferguson, "Auditor General Blasts Liberals' Public-Private Funding and 'High-risk' MaRS Loan," *Toronto Star*, December 9, 2014.

[39] CUPE, "Ours to Keep," op. cit.

[40] The Canadian Press, "Ontario Hydro Auditor's Report Finds Consumers Overcharged By $37 Billion," December 3, 2015.

[41] Elizabeth James, "B.C. Suffering Power Failure," *North Shore News*, May 18, 2011.

[42] Lucille Keen, "Asset Recycling Not Beyond the New Labor," *afr.com*, April 13, 2016.

[43] Cecile Lefort and Byron Kaye, "OMERS Buys Piece of Australia's Busiest Port," *Globe and Mail*, September 19, 2016.

[44] Joyce Nelson, "Bank of Canada Lawsuit," *Watershed Sentinel*, January 11, 2016.

[45] Konrad Yakabuski, "Infrastructure Spending is No Miracle Cure," *Globe & Mail*, April 23, 2015.

[46] Ibid.

[47] Michael Hudson and Gordon Long, "Wall Street Has Taken Over the Economy and Is Draining It," *counterpunch.org*, May 2, 2016.

[48] Barbara Shecter, "CPPIB's Mark Machin to Take Over as CEO Mark Wiseman Departs for Job at BlackRock," *Financial Post*, May 18, 2016.

4. The "New Economy" Czar

[1] Fergal Smith (Reuters), "Bank of Canada Hires Former Merrill Lynch Economist Sheryl King as Adviser," *Financial Post*, May 26, 2016.

[2] Greg Quinn, "Bank of Canada to Expand Ties Within Financial Industry," *Bloomberg News*, May 12, 2016.

[3] Andy Blatchford (CP), "Ottawa's Economic Advisers Gather for First Time with Morneau, Cabinet Ministers," *Ottawa Citizen*, May 15, 2016.

[4] CBC interview, quoted in ibid.

[5] CBC interview, quoted in ibid.

[6] Matt Scuffham and Trevor Hunnicutt, "BlackRock Nabs Canada Pension Chief Wiseman for Senior Role," Reuters, May 19, 2016.

[7] Paul Wells, "Mel Hurtig's Vision a Path not Chosen by Canada: Paul Wells," *Toronto Star,* August 5, 2016.

[8] Andy Blatchford, "Dominic Barton, Canada's New Economy Czar, Calls For 'Aggressive' Change," Canadian Press, May 20, 2016.

[9] Ibid.

[10] Ibid.

[11] Karl Nerenberg, "Morneau Goes Corporate with His New Advisory Council," *rabble.ca,* March 21, 2016.

[12] Ibid.

[13] Ibid.

[14] Ibid.

[15] Gordon Pitts, "Dominic Barton's Global Challenge: Why Mckinsey's New Chief Believes This Could Be Canada's Moment," *Globe and Mail,* August 17, 2009.

[16] Matthew Gwyther, "McKinsey Head Dominic Barton: 'We Don't Dominate the Brain Pool'," *Management Today,* July 10, 2013.

[17] David Rose, "The Firm that Hijacked the NHS: MOS Investigation Reveals Extraordinary Extent of International Management Consultant's Role in Lansley's Health Reforms," *The Mail on Sunday,* February 12, 2012.

[18] Ibid.

[19] Stewart Player and Colin Leys, "McKinsey's Unhealthy Profits," *redpepper.org,* July 2012.

[20] Andrew Gregory, "Top Tory Claims Half of NHS Beds are Facing the Axe Fuelling Fears of Health Privatisation," *Daily Mirror,* October 6, 2015.

[21] Ibid.

[22] Alexandra Sims, Jon Stone, "TTIP has Failed – But No One is Admitting It, says German Vice-Chancellor," *The Independent,* August 28, 2016.

[23] Salem Saif, "When Consultants Reign," *Jacobin Magazine,* May, 2016.

[24] Ibid.

[25] Ibid.

[26] Margot Habiby and Grant Smith, "Saudi Arabia Says Aramco IPO on Track as It Weights Best Approach," *Bloomberg,* August 26, 2016.

[27] Joyce Nelson, "GE and the Privatization of Water," *Watershed Sentinel,* January, 2012.

[28] Joyce Nelson, "High Voltage," *Watershed Sentinel,* September-October, 2011.

[29] Andy Blatchford, "Ottawa's Economic Advisers to Meet Morneau to Discuss Canada's Weak Growth," Canadian Press, August 23, 2016.

5. The Turn-Around Specialist

[1] Dominic Barton, "Capitalism for the Long Term," *Harvard Business Review,* March 2011.

[2] Ibid.

[3] Matt Taibbi, "Looting the Pension Funds," *Rolling Stone,* September 26, 2013.

[4] Jake Johnson, "As Millions of Workers Face Pension Cuts Thanks to Wall Street Greed, Executive Benefits Remain Lavish," *commondreams.org,* April 29, 2016.

[5] Pam Martens and Russ Martens, "Goldman Sachs Doesn't Have Clean Hands in Greece Crisis," *wallstreetonparade.com,* June 30, 2015.

[6] Barton, op. cit.

[7] Suzanna Andrews, "Larry Fink's $12 Trillion Shadow," *Vanity Fair,* April 2010.

[8] Thomas Frank, *Pity The Billionaire: The Hard-Times Swindle and the Unlikely Comeback of the Right,* New York: Henry Holt & Company, 2012, p. 49.

[9] George Monbiot, "Debt Deal: Anger and Deceit Has Led the US Into a Billionaires' Coup," *The Guardian,* August 1, 2011.

[10] Barton, op. cit.

6: Year of Our Overlords 2010

[1] Quoted in Thomas Frank, *Pity the Billionaire,* New York: Henry Holt and Company, 2012, p. 93.

[2] "Killer Capitalist Sentenced to Country Club," *Workers Vanguard,* June 3, 2016.

[3] Ibid.

[4] Michael Lewis, *Flash Boys: A Wall Street Revolt,* New York/London: W.W. Norton & Co., 2014.

[5] Michael Lewis, *The Big Short,* New York/London: W.W. Norton & Co., p. 262.

[6] Matt Taibbi, *The Divide: American Injustice in the Age of the Wealth Gap,* New York: Spiegel &

Grau Trade Paperback, 2014, p. 39.
[7] Lewis, *The Big Short,* p. 262.
[8] Greg Palast, "The Confidential Memo at the Heart of the Global Financial Crisis," *vice.com,* September 10, 2013.
[9] Ibid.
[10] Ibid.
[11] Ibid.
[12] Ibid.
[13] Ibid.
[14] Greg Palast, *Vulture's Picnic,* New York: Penguin Group, 2011, p. 329.
[15] Conn Hallinan, "European Union: A House Divided," *counterpunch.org,* May 23, 2016.
[16] Matt Taibbi, "Obama's Big Sellout: The President has Packed His Economic Team with Wall Street Insiders," *Rolling Stone,* December 13, 2009.
[17] Kim Willsher, "Stephane Hessel, Writer and Inspiration behind Occupy Movement, Dies at 95," *The Guardian,* February 27, 2013.
[18] Stephane Hessel, *Time for Outrage* (English Translation), London: Quartet Books, 2011, p. 23.
[19] Ibid., p. 20.
[20] Ibid.
[21] Ellen Brown, "It's the Interest, Stupid! Why Bankers Rule the World," *truth-out.org,* November 8, 2012.
[22] Hessel, op. cit., p. 23.
[23] Ibid., pp. 22-23.
[24] Dominic Barton, "Capitalism for the Long Term," *Harvard Business Review,* March 2011.
[25] Ibid.
[26] Ibid.
[27] Ibid.
[28] Ibid.
[29] Ibid.

7: Zucotti Park & the Meme Warriors

[1] Naomi Klein, *The Shock Doctrine: The Rise of Disaster Capitalism,* Toronto: Alfred A. Knopf Canada, 2007.
[2] Pamela Heaven, "'Anyone can Make Money in a Market Crash'," *Financial Post,* September 27, 2011.
[3] "Occupy Wall Street Issues Collective Statement by the New York City General Assembly," *The Flying Shingle,* October 10, 2011.
[4] See for example: David Graeber, *The Democracy Project: A History, a Crisis, a Movement,* London: Allen Lane, 2013; Kalle Lasn and Adbusters, *Meme Wars: The Creative Destruction of Neoclassical Economics,* New York: Seven Stories Press, 2012; W. J. T. Mitchell, Bernard Harcourt and Michael Taussig, *Occupy: Three Inquiries in Disobedience,* Chicago: University of Chicago Press, 2013.
[5] Martin Sandbu, "Talkin' 'bout a Revolution," *Financial Times,* April 19, 2013.
[6] Quoted in "Stephane Hessel, The Man Behind Outrage, Protest And Resistance, Will Inspire Forever," *Countercurrents.org,* February 28, 2013.
[7] Linda McQuaig, "Occupy Moves Us into a New Era," *Toronto Star,* November 25, 2011.
[8] Bill Tieleman, "Unlikely Ally of Occupy Movement: Billionaires," *thetyee.ca,* October 18, 2011.
[9] McQuaig, op. cit.
[10] Matt Taibbi, "Wall Street Isn't Winning – It's Cheating," *Rolling Stone,* October 25, 2011.
[11] Ibid.
[12] Nicholas Kristof, "Crony Capitalism Comes Home," The *New York Times,* October 26, 2011.
[13] Ibid.
[14] Pam Martens, "Wall Street Firms Spy on Protesters in Tax-Funded Center," *Wallstreetonparade.com,* October 18, 2011.
[15] Ibid.
[16] Pam Martens, "60 Minutes Takes a Pass on Wall Street's Secret Spy Center," *CounterPunch.org,* February 6, 2012.
[17] Ibid.
[18] Bloomberg Video Excerpt, November 21, 2011, available on Linette Lopez and Robert Johnson,

"You Won't Believe What Bill Gross And Larry Fink Said About Occupy Wall Street On Bloomberg," *Business Insider,* November 22, 2011.
[19] Ibid.
[20] Ibid.
[21] Ibid.
[22] Naomi Wolf, "Revealed: How the FBI Coordinated the Crackdown on Occupy," *The Guardian,* December 29, 2012.
[23] Ibid.
[24] Wikipedia.
[25] Wolf, op. cit.
[26] Ibid.
[27] Lynn Forester de Rothschild and Dominic Barton, "The Case for Inclusive Capitalism," *The Guardian,* May 15, 2012.
[28] Andrew Cave, "London Hosts World Leaders in Debate on 'Fairer' Capitalism," *The Telegraph,* May 26, 2014.
[29] Tom Brooks-Pollock, "'Inclusive Capitalism' Conference Ends in High Court Battle between Organizers," *The Telegraph,* July 24, 2014.

8: COMER & the National Memory

[1] Les Whittington, "Rocco Galati in Court to Challenge How Bank of Canada Does Business," *Toronto Star,* March 24, 2015.
[2] "COMER's Court Case Proceeds: Statement of Claim," *Economic Reform,* January 2012.
[3] Ibid.
[4] Murray Dobbin, "Liberate the Bank of Canada, Intrepid Think Tank Urges," t*hetyee.ca,* April 17, 2015.
[5] Hon. Paul Hellyer, "The Democratization of Money and Banking: An Open Letter to Prime Minister Trudeau," *globalresearch.ca,* June 7, 2016.
[6] Brett Popplewell, "Toronto Revolutionary, 93, Girds for One More Battle," *Toronto Star,* May 17, 2008.
[7] Ibid.
[8] William Krehm, "The Bank of Canada – a Misused Tool," Appendix 1 in William F. Hixson, *It's Your Money,* Toronto: COMER Publications, 1997, p. 125.
[9] Rob Gilroy and Alisa Mamak, "Think You Could Balance a National Budget? Give It a Try," *Globe and Mail,* March 29, 2012.
[10] Ellen Brown, "Canada's 2012 Budget: Imposing Austerity on the World's Most Resource-rich Country," *commondreams.org,* April 1, 2012.
[11] Ibid.
[12] Ibid.
[13] Michael Hudson, Gordon Long, "Wall Street Has Taken Over the Economy and Is Draining It," *counterpunch.org,* May 2, 2016.
[14] Ibid.

9: The EU Flaunts Its Undemocratic Tendencies

[1] Ellen Brown, "A Public Bank Option for Scotland," *truth-out.org,* September 17, 2014.
[2] "EU Commission Seeks to Push Through Free Trade Agreement with Canada (CETA) without Parliamentary Approval," *Deutsche Welle,* June 28, 2016.
[3] Ibid.
[4] Reuters, "EU Commission to Opt for Simple Approval for Canada deal: EU Official," June 28, 2016.
[5] "EU Commission: CETA Should be Approved by National Parliaments," *Deutsche Welle,* July 5, 2016.
[6] The Canadian Press, "Canada-EU Trade Deal to Bring 'Modest' Benefits to Canadian Economy: Reports," *CTV News,* November 6, 2013.
[7] Sean Smith, "Trade Talks with EU Threaten Public Sector, Sovereignty," *CCPA Monitor,* September 2010.
[8] Ibid.
[9] Rick Tufts, "How PM Harper Plans to Sell Out Canada to the International Banking Cartel," *Economic Reform,* May-June, 2014.

[10] Pia Eberhardt, Blair Redlin, Cecile Toubeau, "Trading Away Democracy: How CETA's Investor Protection Rules Threaten the Public Good in Canada and the EU," Council of Canadians et al, November, 2014.

[11] Ibid.

[12] Robert Fife, "Despite Brexit Vote, Key EU Powers Vow to Ratify CETA deal," *Globe and Mail,* July 3, 2016.

[13] Chrystia Freeland, "Plutocrats vs. Populists," *The New York Times,* November 1, 2013.

[14] Op. Cit.

[15] Ibid.

[16] "EU Commission: CETA Should Be Approved by National Parliaments," *Deutsche Welle,* July 5, 2016.

[17] "EC Set to Scrap Plans to Fast-track CETA Deal: Report," *Globe and Mail,* July 5, 2016.

[18] 'Canada Gets Clarity on How Europe will Ratify Trade Deal," *CBC,* July 5, 2016.

[19] Council of Canadians, "CETA to be Considered a 'Mixed Agreement, Now More Vulnerable to Defeat," July 5, 2016.

[20] Council of Canadians, "CETA Vulnerable to Defeat: Council of Canadians," July 5, 2016.

[21] Lawrence Herman, "We Don't Have to Wait for Ratification – Parts of CETA can be Implemented Now," *Globe and Mail,* July 6, 2016.

[22] Lamiat Sabin, "Brexit 'Might Not Stop Awful Ceta'," *Morning Star,* July 5, 2016.

[23] "Barroso and Goldman Sachs – a Dangerous Liaison," *Corporate Europe Observatory,* July 19, 2016.

[24] "As TTIP Falters, Campaigners Warn Against Democracy-Wrecking Sister Deals," *commondreams.org,* August 31, 2016.

[25] Linda McQuaig, "Why is Trudeau Following Harper's Lead and Giving Special Protections to Powerful Corporations?" *Toronto Star,* September 1, 2016.

[26] Andy Blatchford, "Rising Anti-trade Sentiments among G20 Peers Complicates Canada-EU Deal," *Toronto Star,* September 4, 2016.

10: CETA: The "No Lawyers Left Behind" Treaty

[1] Robert Fife, "Despite Brexit Vote, Key EU Powers Vow to Ratify CETA Deal," *Globe and Mail,* July 3, 2016.

[2] Cecilia Malmstrom and Chrystia Freeland, "For Canada and Europe, Now is the Time for Bridges, Not Walls," *Globe and Mail,* July 8, 2016.

[3] Pia Eberhardt, "The Zombie ISDS," Corporate Europe Observatory, March 2016.

[4] Council of Canadians, "CETA Changes Make Investor-state Provisions Worse," February 3, 2016.

[5] Pia Eberhardt and Cecilia Olivet, "Profiting from Injustice," Corporate Europe Observatory, November 27, 2012.

[6] Ibid.

[7] Scott Sinclair, "NAFTA Chapter 11 Investor-State Disputes," Canadian Centre for Policy Alternatives, January 1, 2015.

[8] Maude Barlow, "Fighting TTIP, CETA and ISDS: Lessons from Canada," Council of Canadians, 2015.

[9] Quentin Casey, "'Poor Sister' Has Rich Future," *Financial Post,* March 22, 2013.

[10] Joyce Nelson, "Jumbo: Where Even the Politics Are Wild," *Watershed Sentinel,* September-October, 2012.

[11] Rocco Galati Interview by Michael Welch, "The People's Fighter," *Global Research News Hour,* February 1, 2014.

[12] Bill Curry," "EU could Drop Contentious Clauses from U.S. Talks," *Globe and Mail,* September 30, 2014.

[13] Eberhardt, op. cit.

[14] BJ Siekierski, "'We're Watching UK Referendum Vote Closely': Canada's Chief CETA Negotiator," *iPolitics,* March 10, 2016.

[15] Felix Heilmann, "Goodbye Democracy, Hello CETA?" *stop-TTIP.org,* April 4, 2016.

[16] "Bulgaria Says It will not Ratify CETA," Council of Canadians, May 14, 2016.

[17] Omar Allam, "With CETA in Peril, Canadian Business Needs to Rally behind Ottawa," *Globe and Mail,* July 5, 2016.

[18] Bruce Campion-Smith, "Ball now in Industries' Court after EU Deal," *Toronto Star,* January 2, 2014.

[19] Drew Hasselback, "John Baird joins Bennett Jones as Senior Advisor," *Financial Post*, May 26, 2015.

[20] Stuart Trew, "Profiting from Injustice: New European Report Puts Investor-state Industry Under the Microscope," Council of Canadians, November 27, 2012.

11: The Potential of Postal Banking

[1] Ethan Cox, "Canada Post should Deliver on Postal Banking," *Toronto Star*, February 19, 2014.

[2] "CUPW Demands Release of Canada Post's Postal Banking Study," *cupw.ca*, July 19, 2016.

[3] Cox, op cit.

[4] Jim Bronskill, "Should Canada Post Become A Bank? No Need, Says Banking Lobby," Canadian Press, July 13, 2016.

[5] CUPW, "Big Banks can Lobby All They Want but Postal Banking is Still on the Table: Union," July 13, 2016.

[6] CUPW Fact Sheet, "Postal Banking – A Bank for Everyone," March 2, 2016.

[7] David J. Climenhaga, "It's Time for a National Postal Bank in Both Canada and the United States," *rabble.ca*, May 24, 2016.

[8] Quoted in ibid.

[9] Quoted in ibid.

[10] Quoted in ibid.

[11] John Anderson, "Why Canada Needs Postal Banking," Canadian Centre for Policy Alternatives, October, 2013.

[12] Ibid.

[13] Chris Hedges, "Overthrow the Speculators," *truthdig.com*, December 29, 2013.

[14] Alexandra Bradbury, "When Postmasters Attack," *Labor Notes*, November 26, 2012.

[15] Ryan Maloney, "Maxime Bernier Calls For Canada Post To Be Privatized Amid Labour Dispute," *Huffington Post Canada*, July 8, 2016.

[16] David Camfield, "A Clash of Visions for Public Postal Service: What's at Stake at Canada Post," *rabble.ca*, August 10, 2016.

[17] "Canada Post's Relationship with Workers is Blighted by Underlying Toxicity," *CBC News*, August 27, 2016.

[18] Mike Palecek, "Canada Post is Not on Life Support, It is being Murdered," *rabble.ca*, December 17, 2013.

[19] Simon Goodley, "Royal Mail Privatisation: Goldman Sachs and UBS to be Grilled by MPs," *The Guardian*, November 14, 2013.

[20] Ibid.

[21] Tim Shufelt, "IPO would Help Canada Post Unlock Value," *Globe and Mail*, December 12, 2013.

[22] Evert Hoogers, Donald Swartz, and Rosemary Warskett, "Postal Workers Confront Canada Post: The Struggle Continues in 2016," *Socialist Project*, July 26, 2016; reposted in *Global Research*, July 26, 2016.

[23] Francois Bertrand, Krysyna T. Hoeg, Jim Hopson, Marena McLaughlin, "Canada Post in the Digital Age: Discussion Paper," September 12, 2016.

12: More Crappy Trade Deals: TPP and TISA

[1] Meghan Sali, "TPP Can you Hear Me?" *Watershed Sentinel*, Summer 2016.

[2] Ibid.

[3] "How the Trans-Pacific Partnership Would Impact Financial Regulations," *exposethetpp.org* (undated).

[4] Ibid.

[5] Ibid.

[6] Ibid.

[7] Ibid.

[8] Matt Stannard, "Is the Trans-Pacific Partnership a Danger to Public Banks?" Public Banking Institute, January 29, 2015.

[9] Ibid.

[10] Ibid.

[11] Owen Davis, "Deal: US Banks Get Victories In TPP Agreement, *International Business Times*, October 5, 2015.

[12] Nadia Prupis, "Emails Show TPP 'Collusion' Between Big Banks & Obama Administration,"

commondreams.org, May 27, 2016.

[13] Ibid.

[14] Ibid.

[15] Daniel Tencer, "TPP Trade Deal Proposal Would See CBC, Canada Post Exist Solely For Profit," *Huffington Post*, July 30, 2015.

[16] Ibid.

[17] CUPW, "Trans-Pacific Partnership a theat to public postal service – Not too late to take action," April 14, 2016.

[18] "A Blueprint for Global Privatisation," Global Justice Now, August, 2016.

[19] "As TTIP Falters, Campaigners Warn Against Democracy-Wrecking Sister Deals," *commondreams.org*, August 31, 2016.

[20] Scott Sinclair and Hadrien Mertins-Kirkwood, "TISA Versus Public Services," *Public Services International*, April 28, 2014.

[21] Ellen Brown, "Awesome Power Is on the Verge of Being Handed Over to Private Banks if TPP Passes," *Economic Reform*, November-December 2015.

[22] "Booting Corporate Power, Communities Are Taking Back Control of Their Water," *commondreams.org*, April 14, 2015.

[23] Council of Canadians, "Barlow challenges TISA in Switzerland," May 10, 2016.

[24] Ibid.

[25] Brown, op. cit.

[26] Pete Dolack, "Regulation of Financial Industry is History if Trade in Services Agreement Passes," *counterpunch.org*, June 10, 2016.

[27] Ibid.

[28] Ibid.

[29] ''As TTIP Falters, Campaigners Warn Against Democracy-Wrecking Sister Deals," *commondreams.org.*, August 31, 2016.

[30] Dolack, op. cit.

[31] "A Blueprint for Global Privatisation," op. cit.

[32] Quoted in Eric Zuesse, "TTP, TTIP, TISA and CETA: U.N. Legal Expert Calls Proposed Trade Deals 'Illegal'," *globalresearch.ca*, June 25, 2016.

[33] "UN Expert Urges Pacific Rim Countries Not to Sign the TPP without Committing to Human Rights and Development," UN Independent Experts, February 3, 2016.

[34] Quoted in Zuesse, op. cit.

13: Hillary, Larry & Dominic: More Looting Opportunities

[1] Zaid Jilani, "Donald Trump and Hillary Clinton Would Be Equally Good for Finance Industry, Says Top Executive," *The Intercept*, June 17, 2016.

[2] Quoted in ibid.

[3] Ibid.

[4] Terry Duffy, "Wall Street Is Losing the Best and Brightest," *Wall Street Journal*, September 30, 2013.

[5] Ibid.

[6] Jilani, op. cit.

[7] Charlie Gasparino and Julie VerHage, "BlackRock's Fink Hoping Hillary is Ticket to Treasury Post," *Fox Business News*, January 21, 2014.

[8] Ibid.

[9] Andrew Gavin Marshall, "Exposing BlackRock: Who's Afraid of Laurence Fink and His Overpowering Institution?" *occupy.com*, December 23, 2015.

[10] "Wall Street CEO sounds a lot like Hillary Clinton," *money.cnn.com*, February 3, 2016.

[11] Stephen Gandel, "BlackRock's Larry Fink May Be Steppping Up His Play for Treasury Secretary," *Fortune*, February 4, 2016.

[12] David Dayen, "Larry Fink and His BlackRock Team Posed to Take Over Hillary Clinton's Treasury Department," *The Intercept*, March 2, 2016.

[13] Ibid.

[14] Ibid.

[15] Ibid.

[16] Yves Smith, "Social Security Privatizer Larry Fink of Giant Asset Manager BlackRock is a Clinton Treasury Secretary in Waiting," *nakedcapitalism.com*, March 3, 2016.

[17] Ibid.

[18] Andrew Coyne, "Andrew Coyne: 'Turning the CPP into 18 Million 'RRSPs'," *National Post,* July 11, 2016.

[19] "It's Time to Close the Retirement Advice Loophole," undated, *SaveOurRetirment.com.*

[20] Maxine Waters, "Every Moment We Delay Further Depletes Americans' Meager Retirement Savings," Committee Statement, October 27, 2015.

[21] Insured Retirement Institute Board of Directors, *irionline.org.*

[22] Myles Udland, "Hillary: Corporate America is Obsessed with 'Quarterly Capitalism' – and Here's How I'd Change That," *Business Insider,* June 14, 2016.

[23] Quoted in Jon Schwartz, "Hillary Clinton Hints at Giant, Trump-like Giveaway to Corporate America," *The Intercept,* June 27, 2016.

[24] Jennifer Wells, "Clinton's Economic Plan an Economy Boosting Balance," *Toronto Star,* August 14, 2016.

[25] Norman Solomon, "Clinton's Transition Team: a Corporate Presidency Foretold," *counterpunch. org,* August 22, 2016.

[26] Jonathan Stempel, "Wall Street to Privatize US Infrastructure," *globalresearch,ca,* August 3, 2008.

[27] Nicolas Van Praet, "Caisse Eyes U.S. Infrastructure Projects," *Globe and Mail,* February 26, 2015.

[28] "Infrastructure Rising," BlackRock, April 2015, p. 10.

[29] Chris Edwards, "Privatization," *downsizinggovernment.org,* July 12, 2016.

[30] Mitchell Anderson, "The Verdict on Thatcherism Is Clear," *thetyee.ca,* October 3, 2014.

[31] Edwards, op. cit.

[32] Oliver Milman, "The Political Crusaders Targeting National Parks for Drilling and Exploitation," *The Guardian,* August 23, 2016.

[33] Chris Hedges and Michael Hudson, "The Lies of Neoliberal Economics (or How America Became a Nation of Sharecroppers)," *counterpunch.org,* April 1, 2016.

[34] Ibid.

[35] Barbara Schecter, "Mark Jenkins is Leaving CPPIB, Triggering Executive Shakeup at Pension Manager," *Financial Post,* September 12, 2016.

[36] Paul Wells, "One-stop Shopping the Goal for Potential International Investors," *Toronto Star,* September 14, 2016.

[37] Ibid.

[38] Ibid.

14: Bilderberg & "The Wake Behind the Shark Fin"

[1] Andrew Coyne, "Andrew Coyne: Funding Government Projects through Public Pension Plans a Terrible Idea," *National Post,* April 25, 2016.

[2] Reuters, "Canada to Target Pension Funds for Infrastructure Funding: Trudeau," June 8, 2016.

[3] Ibid.

[4] Charlie Skelton, "Bilderberg 2012: Ken Clarke's Drive of Shame," *The Guardian,* June 4, 2012.

[5] Charlie Skelton, "Bilderberg 2012: the Technocrats are Rising at This Year's Annual Conference," *The Guardian,* May 30, 2012.

[6] Jean Charest, "Government must Create Conditions for Private Infrastructure Spending," *Globe and Mail,* May 17, 2016.

[7] Ibid.

[8] Ibid.

[9] Joyce Nelson, "The Rockefeller Files: Ontario Election and Privatization," *rabble.ca,* June 6, 2014.

[10] Matt Scuffham, "Caisse Ups Stakes in Montreal Transit Investment," *Globe and Mail,* September 19, 2016.

[11] Natalie Mehra, "If the Wynne Government can Privatize Hydro One, Even Though It will Drive Up Costs for Ontarians and Businesses, What's Next?" *Economic Reform,* September-October, 2015.

[12] CUPE, "Time for Police to Investigate Hydro One Sale," March 30, 2016.

[13] Adrian Morrow, "An Inside Look at Cash-for-access Ontario Liberal Fundraisers," *Globe and Mail,* July 6, 2016.

[14] CUPE, op. cit.

[15] The Canadian Press, "CUPE sues Ontario Liberals in an Effort to Block the Sale of Any More Hydro One Shares," *National Post*, September 14, 2016.

[16] Peter Levring and Christian Wienberg, "In Denmark, Goldman Sachs Deal Ignites Political Crisis," *Business Week*, February 6, 2014.

[17] Jonas Schmidt Hansen, "Ding-Dong! Goldman Sachs Just Ate Denmark For Breakfast," *occupy.com*, June 13, 2016.

[18] Matthew Yglesias, "Dong Energy Deal Has Danish Government on the Brink of Collapse," *Slate*, January 30, 2014.

[19] Schmidt Hansen, op. cit.

[20] Ibid.

[21] Ibid.

[22] Ibid.

[23] Ibid.

15: Are Pipeline P3s in the Agenda?

[1] Brian Porter, "Getting the Long View Right," *scotiabank.com*, February 12, 2016.

[2] Ibid.

[3] "Scotiabank CEO Says Federal Infrastructure Dunds should be Spent on Energy East Pipeline," Council of Canadians, February 12, 2016.

[4] Amy MacPherson, "Where Your CPP Money Really Goes: Part 2," *Huffington Post*, January 22, 2013.

[5] Hamish Stewart, "Hamish Stewart: The Canada Pension Plan's Love Affair with Big Oil," *nationalobserver.com*, August 8, 2016.

[6] Rainforest Action Network, Sierra Club, BankTrack, Oil Change International, "Shorting the Climate: Fossil Fuel Finance Report Card 2016," Spring, 2016.

[7] Reuters, "Canada's Pension Funds Eye Greenfield Federal Infrastructure Investments," *Financial Post*, July 6, 2016.

[8] "New Thinking: Canada's Roadmap to Smart Prosperity," *Sustainable Prosperity.ca*, February 2016, p. 8.

[9] Ibid., p. 22.

[10] Ibid., p. 11.

[11] Gordon Pitts, "Dominic Barton's Global Challenge: Why McKinsey's New Chief Believes This could be Canada's Moment," *Globe and Mail,* August 17, 2009.

[12] Dominic Barton, "The City and Capitalism for the Long Term," McKinsey & Company, May 15, 2013.

[13] "Shutting the Spigot on Private Water: The Case for the World Bank to Divest," Corporate Accountability International, April, 2012.

[14] Jo-Shing Yang, "The New 'Water Barons': Wall Street Mega-Banks are Buying up the World's Water," *Market Oracle*, December 21, 2012.

[15] "Thematic Investing," Bank of America Merrill Lynch, November 25, 2014.

[16] Quoted in "Barlow Refutes Bulk Water Export Advocate on CBC Radio's The Current," Council of Canadians, May 20, 2016.

[17] Jennifer O'Keeffe, "Turning off the Tap: Site C and Water Privatization in Canada," *globalresearch.ca*, August 9, 2016.

[18] Ibid.

[19] John Calvert, "BC Hydro's Amazingly Bad Deal for Ratepayers," *thetyee.ca*, October 30, 2006.

[20] Damien Gilis, "The $55 Billion Private Power Racket and the Real Story Behind Hydro's Debt," *commonnensecanadian.ca*, July 3, 2013.

[21] Gordon Hamilton, "Shell Switches to Recycled Water for Dawson Creek Fracking," *Vancouver Sun*, September 8, 2012.

[22] Andrew Nikiforuk, "Closure of Lauded Munk School Water Program 'Distressing,' Experts Say," *thetyee.ca* April 19, 2016.

[23] Ibid.

[24] Ibid.

[25] Council on Foreign Relations, "North America: Time For a New Focus," October, 2014.

[26] Scott Smith, "Federal, State Leaders Pitch for California Water Tunnels," *The Republic*, July 26, 2016.

16: Lessons from Iceland

[1] John Perkins, *Confessions of an Economic Hit Man,* New York: Penguin Group, 2004.

[2] John Perkins, *Hoodwinked,* New York: Random House, 2009, p. 3.

[3] "Dam Construction in Manitoba to Power Energy East Pipeline," Council of Canadians, May 24, 2014.

[4] Perkins, *Hoodwinked,* op. cit., p. 2

[5] Susan DeMuth, "Power Driven," *The Guardian,* November 29, 2003.

[6] Perkins, *Hoodwinked,* op. cit., p. 3.

[7] Balazs Koranyi, "Iceland a Model of Recovery," *Financial Post,* June 13, 2012.

[8] Michael Lewis, *Boomerang: Travels in the New Third World,* New York & London: W.W. Norton and Company, 2011, p. 3

[9] Quoted in Ellen Brown, "EU/IMF Revolt: Greece, Iceland, Latvia May Lead the Way," *webofdebt.com,* December 7, 2009.

[10] Michael Nevradakis, "An Economic Hit Man Speaks Out: John Perkins on How Greece Has Fallen Victim to 'Economic Hit Men'," *truth-out.org,* September 11, 2014.

[11] Geoff Olson, "This Island Earth," *Common Ground,* June 2013.

[12] Rebecca Savastio, "Icelanders Overthrow Government and Rewrite Constitution After Banking Fraud - No Word from US Media," *Guardianlv.com,* December 2, 2013.

[13] Macedonian International News Agency, "Iceland: They Jailed The Crooked Bankers, Now Every Icelander Will Receive A Payout from the Bank Sale," *globalresearch.ca,* November 22, 2015.

[14] "Iceland's Capital-Controls saga," *The Economist,* June 10, 2015.

[15] Ibid.

[16] Koranyi, op. cit.

[17] Saving Iceland blog post, July 7, 2015.

[18] "Historian and Political Newcomer Gudni Johannesson has Won Iceland's Presidential Election," *BBC News,* June 26, 2016.

[19] "Iceland's Way," *Economic Reform,* November-December, 2015.

[20] Ellen H. Brown, "Reinventing Banking: From Russia to Iceland to Ecuador," *nsnbc international,* December 12, 2015.

[21] Raul Hargi Meijer, "Iceland Stuns Banks: Plans to Take Back the Power to Create Money," *globalresearch.ca,* April 13, 2015.

[22] Lewis, op. cit., p. 23.

Conclusion

[1] J. Baglow, "Liberals' 'Sunny Ways' Eclipsed by Cynical Old-style Ppolitics," *rabble.ca,* July 4, 2016.

[2] David Christopher, "Our Last, Best Chance to Restore our Rights and Repeal Bill C-51," *rabble.ca,* August 1, 2016.

[3] Tonda Maccharles, "CSIS Used Bill C-51 Powers Several Times to Disrupt Suspected Terrorists, Senate Hears," *Toronto Star,* March 7, 2016.

[4] Lawrence Martin, "Anti-terrorism Law: Why the Liberals aren't Living Up to Vow to Amend it," *Globe and Mail, August 2, 2016.*

[5] Fram Dinshaw, "Bill C-51 and 'Fascist Shift' in Canada Decried at Toronto Rally," *National Observer,* May 3, 2015.

[6] "Rocco Galati Plans to Take the Fight Against C-51 to Court," *Press For Truth,* May 31, 2015.

[7] Joyce Nelson, "Police State Canada?" *counterpunch.org,* March 13, 2015.

[8] Quoted in ibid.

[9] Ibid.

[10] Chris Hedges, *Wages of Rebellion: The Moral Imperative of Revolt,* Toronto: Vintage Canada, 2016 (paperback edition), p. 226.

[11] Larry Elliott, "Richest 62 People as Wealthy as Half of World's Population, says Oxfam," *The Guardian,* January 18, 2016.

[12] Vaughn Palmer, "Vaughn Palmer: Trudeau Begins Premier's 'Get-to-yes' Goal with Site C Permits," *Vancouver Sun,* July 29, 2016.

[13] Rodgers Oil and Gas Consulting, "Alberta Royalty Policy and the Notion of In-trust as a Principle of Natural Resources management," *Royalty Review Issues Summary,* January 2016, pp. 8, 3.

[14] John Perkins, *The Secret History of the American Empire,* New York: Penguin Books, 2007, p. 224.

Index

W

[Created with TExtract / www.Texyz.
    com]

About the Author

Joyce Nelson is the author of five previous books – *The Perfect Machine: TV in the Nuclear Age; The Colonized Eye: Rethinking the Grierson Legend; Sultans of Sleaze: PR & The Media; Sign Crimes/Road Kill;* and *Seeing in the Dark* – a poetry book that was a finalist for the B.C. Poetry Prize. As well, she has written hundreds of articles and essays published in a wide range of magazines, newspapers and websites. Her written work has been anthologized in several published collections in both Canada and the U.S.

She was given an award for her writing by the Vancouver Island Human Rights Society and on three occasions her articles have been selected by Project Censored Canada (now NewsWatch Canada) for their Top Ten "significant but under-reported" stories of the year.

Nelson has also created 23 hours of radio documentary for *CBC Ideas*, all of which were re-broadcast by popular demand, and she won 2nd Prize for Radio Drama in the CBC Literary Competition. She is also a visual artist, working in acrylic and water colour.

Nelson has taught at Queen's University and the University of Victoria. She currently writes for the *Watershed Sentinel, counterpunch.org* and other publications, and lives in Toronto, Canada.

See *www.joycenelson.ca*